Critical Thinking

What You Should Have Been Taught About Decision-Making, Problem Solving, Cognitive Biases, Logical Fallacies and Winning Arguments

Contents

Part 1: Critical Thinking

An Essential Guide to Improving Your Decision-Making Skills and Problem-Solving Abilities along with Avoiding Logical Fallacies and Cognitive Biases

Introduction

The human mind is quite a remarkable thing. It is capable of so much, and we have barely tapped into its full potential and what it can really do. Yet, for all its abilities, it can also be a dangerous thing. If you don't know how to keep your thoughts under control or how to leverage that brain of yours to seek truths, you will find yourself making the wrong choices more often than not.

This book aims to disambiguate a lot of the mysteries surrounding the human mind and how it works. People have different beliefs and ideologies, and they are often quite passionate about defending them and proving they are right. Yet, if you looked carefully into a lot of the claims presented by those people you would often find that their logic is flawed, and their reasoning is false. This is because most of us aren't trained to think about everything around us critically. We rarely stop to consider the facts and evidence behind a claim carefully, and we let our personal biases guide us and deliver the eventual conclusion. This is why a lot of people have trouble with decision making and problem-solving, because we find ourselves uncertain and doubtful about whether our decisions are the right ones.

So, what is critical thinking, and why is it so important in life? What would a businessperson or a doctor do with critical thinking? Well, a lot. It is how you should handle any problem or issue in your daily life, from where to eat lunch that day to what is the best course of action for your business. Critical thinking is how you identify biases in yourself, and people around you, and how you can deal with them. Critical thinking will help you understand how people form their beliefs and why they can be so precious and valuable to them.

In this book, you will learn the secrets to critical thinking and how it can change your life, making you a better leader and a person with a greater understanding of the world and the people around you. This book presents expert insights which will guide you into how you should handle the tough decisions you come across so often in your life, and updated tips and hacks to help you solve any problem you encounter. You will find examples of things you probably do that are impairing your judgment and hindering your life without you even knowing it.

At the end of the day, though, changing your mindset is not easy, and it will take a lot of effort and dedication on your part to change your core beliefs and become more accepting of differences and hard truths. The rewards are certainly worth it because you will be an improved version of yourself, one that is persuasive and intellectual rather than impulsive and hesitant. The question is, are you willing to put in the effort to become that person? If so, read on.

Chapter One: How Humans Think

That is the big question, isn't it? How exactly do our minds work? Why do you enjoy a movie, while your friend hates it? How come you have a firm belief system that is different from that of your family? What exactly is it that makes us tick? These are all questions that you have most likely considered if you are reading this book, and they are very valid ones. While there are plenty of psychological factors affecting all these questions, there are also biological ones that we cannot control. "How do humans think?" has been a topic and a question that has baffled scientists and philosophers for centuries, and we've only just scratched the tip of the iceberg.

Philosophy and the Brain over the Years

Yes, advancements in understanding the connection between our brains and how we think and feel have been made recently, but this topic has been contested by philosophers and scientists for centuries. Their views and theories, while often factually incorrect, helped us get where we are now and laid the foundations for what we know today as neurosciences.

Ancient Egyptians believed that it was the heart that was responsible for a human's intellect and the center of their emotions, which is why they left it there during mummification. (The brain, on the other hand, was removed.) Centuries later, Aristotle backed the view that the heart was the seat of intelligence and the reason we are sentient beings; he actually believed that the brain was basically responsible for cooling the blood. Plato, on the other hand, believed that it was the mind that was responsible for the rational thinking we possess. He thought it was the source from which we take actions and think for ourselves.

As time went by, philosophers came and went, each with their different views on the big question of how humans think. Some were completely off the mark, while others were getting close to the real answer, which is the fact that it is our brains that guide us to act and feel how we do.

How the Brain Works

Without getting too technical, it is a given that it is the brain that regulates how we experience and feel things (contrary to popular belief, your heart has no direct relation with who you love or hate). To dive a bit deeper into this, let's talk about the specific parts of your brain that affect certain cognitive functions. Before we get into the specifics, you should be aware of the fact that the human brain is layered, like you see in photos and in movies. Each of those different layers serves a different function, and some of those layers have been in mammalian species from the beginning.

The Old Brain

This is one aspect of the brain that we share with animals, generally speaking, and it is one that our ancestors possessed thousands of years ago. Obviously, evolution runs its course, and we have managed to develop further layers of the brain that led to more sophisticated functions and more complex emotions, but the old brain remains intact, and it will probably always remain so in all mammal species. So, what exactly does it do?

Well, the old brain regulates the functions that your body needs to perform in order to survive. This includes everything from breathing, eating, and sleeping to maintaining a heartbeat. It is basically preprogrammed to take care of our motor actions and basic functions that we need to survive.

The Cerebral Cortex

Basic survival functions aside, it is the cerebral cortex that is responsible for your consciousness and thinking patterns. It is that thin layer of the brain that makes us smarter than all the animals out there, and it is what sets humans apart from any other species. It is why we are much smarter than any of the other animals considered to be intelligent life forms.

The cerebral cortex is a thin layer that looks like bark, covering the outer portion of your brain. It is covered by grey matter – "*meninges*"- which has that color because the nerves around that part of your brain don't have the insulation that is normally present on nerves throughout the rest of your brain, and this makes the nerves appear white. The cerebral cortex allows us to learn and use languages to communicate – a quality largely absent in other mammalian species – and it allows us to acquire intricate skills that no other species can learn. The cerebral cortex is also responsible for our wanting to socialize and be around people. The shape and size of our cerebral cortex make it possible for humans to learn complex, often intangible concepts, and think for themselves in terms above and beyond the primitive instincts that drive other less sophisticated mammals.

The Nervous System

Your body's central nervous system includes the brain, its cerebral cortex, and the spinal cord. You should know that the brain is divided into several lobes, each serving a different function. The Frontal Lobe is responsible for your higher-level cognition, motor skills manifesting in movements and reflexes, and expressive language. The Occipital Lobe is responsible for interpreting any visual stimuli that your brain receives. The Temporal Lobe, on the other hand, is the one that processes sound and interprets the languages we hear, and it is also responsible for memory processing.

The last of them is the Parietal Lobe, which interprets sensory information that you experience physically like touch, pain, pressure, and so on.

These are the basic components of your brain and their areas of expertise. But that still hasn't directly answered our main question, "How does the human brain work?" Well, there is no clear answer to this question, really. Despite the many discoveries made over the years, scientists are still baffled by the specifics of how our brain chooses to think about something in particular as opposed to something else. We simply just know what areas of the brain are responsible for thinking, rationality, vision, and so on, as explained above. For instance, we know that the visual cortex within the occipital lobe uses a lot more energy when you are thinking about something colorful, like some cherry-vanilla ice cream. But it is the sensory cortex within the parietal lobe that lights up when you think about the taste and feel of that ice cream. This is the nature of our knowledge when it comes to how the brain works.

Cognitive Spaces

Despite so much mystery surrounding the human thought process, there are some assumptions in place that do make sense. Scientists believe that the human brain stores all the information it receives and categorizes it components in mental maps of sorts, called cognitive spaces. It is in those spaces located inside the brain where we arrange our past experiences based on factors like geographical data or spatial connections between the different items stored within the cognitive space, as explained by Christian Doeller, a leading scientist advocating this theory. This happens because of the tendency of everything we come across as humans to have some sort of physical properties, one way or another. This means we can arrange them within the mind's cognitive spaces.

Think of it this way; you organize your loved ones, for instance, based on several factors inside your cognitive space. Say you think of your family members in terms of age, height, weight, body structure, etc. You would do the same with laptops; for instance, you would categorize them based on processing speed, screen resolution, materials quality, and so on. Cognitive space is basically your brain's way of coding the input it receives into logical information chunks. The brain puts the data sharing certain dimensions into the same particular spaces. Similar interests would be, therefore, arranged in the same cognitive spaces.

Neuroplasticity

One more thing you should learn about to understand how the human mind works is neuroplasticity. Ever asked yourself why it is much easier to learn a new language or how to play an instrument at a younger age than it is when you are an adult? Sure, stresses of adulthood and not having as much free time do make a difference, but the biggest deciding factor actually has to do with your brain, and how it functions. Neuroplasticity is the brain's ability to adapt to new surroundings and conditions, and its ability to change its structure and functions in response to such changes, even in response to damage that parts of your body or the brain itself might have sustained.

The brain isn't rigid, but rather flexible and constantly adapting, and is capable of adjusting its settings to take in new data while adapting to varying circumstances. It is because of neuroplasticity that a right-handed person who lost their right arm gradually learns to use their left arm until they become equally adept with it. This happens because the brain rewires its settings to adjust to these new circumstances by creating different neural-communication routes. This also happens when you're trying to learn a new language or skill. It is much easier for children to learn and adapt because our brains are at their most flexible at a young age. Those neural communication routes are still being formed and developed, so it is much easier for kids to learn; hence the saying, "a child's brain is like a sponge".

Still, neuroplasticity continues to play a significant role in our evolution even as adults, and your brain is constantly rewiring its settings to deal with any changes it encounters on a regular basis. For instance, talented musicians' brains work differently than ours -- they have large auditory cortexes as opposed to a normal person, as shown in a study in 2005 by Bengtsson et al. This is a clear example of neuroplasticity and how the brain adjusts certain wirings so it could serve a person's particular circumstance.

There is much to be said, and more importantly explored, when it comes to how our minds work. We have barely unraveled just what the brain is capable of, and there's so much that we will still discover in the years to come. What you need to understand right now, for the purposes of this book, is that your brain is divided into several active parts, and each is responsible for a certain function or role.

Chapter Two: Critical Thinking: Uses, Skills, and Benefits

You would be hard-pressed to find someone who hasn't come across the term "critical thinking" in one way or another. But what exactly does it mean, and why is it a good thing? Is it even a good thing, or is it just a way to add more stress to an already overtaxed mind? These and many more questions on critical thinking will be answered in this chapter.

What is Critical Thinking?

Contrary to popular belief, critical thinking does not necessarily mean criticizing (though you might be able to do that much more effectively after engaging in critical thinking). It is simply a way of absorbing information and inputs coming in from different places, analyzing them, and thinking them over before trying to form an opinion. This is basically what the term means.

It is how you rationally entertain thoughts and arguments, without rushing to form an opinion and pass judgment. You need to be able to critically think independently of how others tell you to think because this is how you come to truly form your own beliefs and convictions rather than just repeating others'. Much of the problems we're facing in the world today -the hatred, intolerance, bigotry, xenophobia, anger, and much more- would simply vanish if people learned to think for themselves. A person isn't born a racist or homophobic; they inherit those notions from the societies in which they dwell, and they never stop to think them over.

Why do You Need Critical Thinking?

Why is it then that it is important to have this analytical approach to everything -- to carefully consider and think about the claims and arguments you hear every day, especially in the age of the internet?

Forming Your Own Beliefs

Let's face it; we're all born into a certain doctrine, whether religious, societal, or other. Critical thinking helps you question each and every one of those doctrines and decide for yourself whether that is really something that you have to follow. There's nothing wrong with following a certain religion or becoming an atheist; it's the people who follow either path without thinking it over, just because they were told this is the right way, that all too often pose some form of threat. You won't find a religious fanatic or racist practicing critical thinking; they're pretty much just misled people who never take the time to think for themselves.

When you critically think things over, you will never fall into those categories. You will never harbor hate towards another person because of their sex, color, creed, religion, or any other reason. You will start finding things that connect you to people rather than set you apart.

A Better Understanding of Things

Critical thinking allows you to form a better understanding of things in general. Acquiring knowledge is never really about accumulating as much information as you can; any person with a good memory could do that. But what good is that knowledge if you don't think about it and analyze it? Acquiring knowledge is about analyzing the inputs you get, finding correlation and/or causation, and deducing the consequences of a particular piece of information or argument. Then, this will help you put that knowledge to good use, and you will be able to use it to solve problems and answer bigger and more important questions.

You will find that all scientists and great thinkers of our time and times past lived by a code to critically question everything. They constructed and deconstructed whatever information, claims, or hypotheses they heard, and this allowed them to have a significantly better understanding of our universe. Critical thinking also allows you to understand the logical connection between ideas and how everything is connected, which is the foundation on which science is based.

The Rationality of Forming an Argument

We live in an age where people argue about everything; some people even argue for a living. It is quite easy to come off as uninformed or foolish in such times, and this is why you need critical thinking. It will allow you to understand one very important point that could change your life: *it is not about being right or wrong or passing judgment*, except in cases where it is clear and simple enough to pass such judgments, known as a "black-and-white" case. Once you fully grasp the notion that you don't need to render a judgment on everything, but rather analyze and understand each and every claim from all angles, you will start reacting differently and more rationally.

Then, if and when you do want to form an argument, you will be able to do it from a rational point of view that is based on being informed and reasonable rather than just impulsive. You will be able to further your claims and explain why you disagree with sound arguments rather than using the "I'm right, you're wrong" approach, which is often futile and doesn't really help or contribute to making a change in any way. Which brings us to a very important usage of critical thinking: problem-solving. As we will explore later in the book, one of the main reasons why a lot of people have trouble with problem-solving is because they rarely approach the matter at hand critically.

Becoming a Better Person

Critical thinking will simply help you become a better person. You will develop more empathy and start to come to the realization that you don't have to be right all the time; maybe the other person is right sometimes. Maybe your view of the world isn't the only valid one, and perhaps there is a different reality outside of the confinements of the box you're in. You start empathizing with others, and you see other points of view for what they truly are; just viewpoints of people who don't share your beliefs, not enemies or people you should be hating on for being different. Critical thinking helps you see beyond the cultural norms and view people for who they are rather than who you're told they are. This, and the fact that you shed all hate towards those that are merely different, helps you become a better person and a better leader, which brings us to the next point.

Improving as a Leader

Reading this, you might be asking yourself, still, how does critical thinking help me? Well, it will help you become a much better leader and manager. The empathy you gain from analyzing and thinking about other people's points of view means you will be able to show those ideas the respect and recognition they deserve. It also means that you will be better equipped when it comes to decision-making because you understand that each problem needs to be considered from all angles. When a team member talks to you about a problem they're facing, you won't get defensive and start undermining their problem; instead, you will listen and think it over, and you might find that they have a valid complaint.

If one of your team members suggests an idea and you critically think about it, your ego will never get in the way. If it is indeed a good idea, you will embrace it and push your people forward, because you will simply see that it is good for business, and what's good for business is good for you. Critical thinking will also help you communicate better, as each point or claim you make will be backed by evidence and sound reasoning rather than emotions. This will help you reach your subordinates and deliver your messages elaborately and clearly.

Business and Science

What do those two disciplines have in common? Both rely heavily on critical thinking, and it has played and will play a significant role in their evolution. When you start considering problems from all angles and thinking of your possible choices and solutions, you will become a much better problem-solver, which is a must for any professional in this day and age. Critical thinking also promotes creativity, because that is what it takes to find a solution to a tricky problem that you have considered from all angles. You won't just settle with an ordinary answer, because you will keep analyzing your solution and finding different ways to improve it.

As for science, it goes without saying that all scientific theories and experimentation are based on critical thinking. Scientists question everything, and their theories and hypotheses aren't based on just their intellectual abilities but rather on how they are able to construct their reasoning and connect ideas.

Making Sense of the World

All the previous points aside, we need critical thinking to make sense of the world, especially in such a polarized one as ours today. You're constantly being told what's right and what's wrong, who the bad people are that you should hate; it can be a very slippery slope to take everything you hear as the truth without subjecting the claims to reason and critical thinking. Critical thinking is how you will be able to determine which claims are correct, and which are false and biased, possibly serving a particular agenda.

You keep hearing the term "false news," but is it false news? And if so, why is that? This is where critical thinking comes in; it's your way of knowing what makes sense and what doesn't, and more importantly, how you should act on it. Some philosophers say that there are no absolute truths, but if there were, critical thinking is how you would find them.

Does Critical Thinking Go Against Personal Beliefs and Feelings?

No, it does not. Critical thinking simply means that the arguments you form and your approach to problem-solving aren't going to be based on faith, personal beliefs, or gut feelings, but rather sensible and rational consideration of the facts presented and the available information. If you want to call a person an idiot rather than show why they're wrong, at least do it while providing a reason as to why they are idiots (though it really doesn't help your case if you start with name-calling).

Chapter Three: Critical Thinking Mental Models

Now that you understand what critical thinking is, and what its benefits are, we get to the tricky part. Yes, all the above was basically an introduction to critical thinking. Now, the real deal is, how do you practice this thinking technique? Learning to do it isn't hard, but it is also far from easy or simple. This is not because learning to think critically is complicated per se, but rather because it takes self-discipline and a clear mind to do it.

So, how can you do it? Well, the good news is, there are thousands of different ways to model your thinking. But that is also the bad news. The mental models we are going to explore throughout this chapter are simply ways to explain or think about a certain topic in regard to how it works. It is a concept or a framework within your own mind that will help you explain things and understand the meaning behind them. In this chapter, we are going to explore some of the most important ones out there, but you should know that there are thousands of existing mental models, each discipline in life having its own set that can be learned and applied. You already know this; take supply-and-demand, for instance. It is a mental model that helps you understand how the economy operates and the factors influencing it. Relativity is a mental model that explains the laws of nature like gravity and the cosmos around us.

Occam's Razor

This is the first of the mental models we are going to be exploring. Occam's razor is quite simple, really; it states that when encountering a problem or something that needs explaining, the simplest and most direct of your explanations/answers is often the right one.

This is an approach to follow when you get several competing hypotheses to a dilemma. In such cases, the one that requires making the least assumptions to prove its correctness is the right hypothesis. You should know, though, that this approach is to be followed with hypotheses explaining the same occurrence, so it shouldn't be used to explain competing points of view. In other words, your explanations have to come to the same conclusion or prediction, but that doesn't mean they are all correct.

So, let's say you woke up one morning to find your car parked in the street but covered in dirt. You have a couple of explanations for that incident. The heavy rain from the previous night might have splashed up dirt on your car. Or the neighborhood kids may have conspired against you, gathered some mud in a bucket, and slipped undetected in the rain to your car to throw mud at it. As you can see, the outcome is the same; your car is dirty. But the hypotheses are completely different. In this scenario, the obvious likely explanation is the first, because it requires fewer assumptions.

If you ran out of gas on your way to work, the most likely reason is that you forgot to fill the tank the day before, not the existence of a gas-stealing gang that sneaked into your closed garage at nightfall and emptied your tank. Again, the same outcome, but Occam's Razor contends that the explanation with the least number of assumptions is the more likely one.

Hanlon's Razor

This is another proverb or way of thinking to explain some human behaviors, and it is definitely inspired by Occam's razor. It goes like this: "Never attribute to malice that which can be adequately explained by stupidity." This is perhaps one of the most useful approaches to critical thinking because it's one that could help us avoid a lot of unnecessary conflicts.

Hanlon's Razor simply means that sometimes bad things happen, but that doesn't necessarily imply evil intentions. Sometimes, the other person is just stupid or incompetent, or they simply didn't think it through. In other words, not everyone's your enemy and people aren't out to get you.

Your colleague at work didn't spill coffee on your favorite shirt because they hate you; they did it accidentally, without meaning you any ill will. The random person who rear-ended you in the street isn't out to crash into all BMW car owners; they just lost focus for a second or were too tired after a long day at work.

Just imagine the kind of world we'd be living in if people weren't constantly hostile and assuming the worst. Hanlon's Razor is a simple mental model that teaches you that you shouldn't always assume the worst from people's behaviors. Simply put, give people the benefit of the doubt; you'll be surprised how much less stressful and happier your life and theirs will be.

First-Principle Reasoning

First-principle reasoning is one of the most important mental models out there and is particularly suited to scientific disciplines. First-principle thinking is a way to try to reach absolute truth, if such a thing exists.

A first principle is an idea, notion, or assumption that stands on its own merit, as it cannot be deduced from any other assumptions or theories. Aristotle was the first one to come up with this concept, asserting that it could help us know everything we need to know simply because we know the basic truth. When you use first-principles reasoning, you ignore all other false assumptions, models, conventions, and thoughts that cloud your judgment and impair your quest for the truth. There is only the basic first principle, which you will try to find by asking the right powerful questions.

So, how do you practice first-principle reasoning? In a nutshell, question everything. Don't take any answers for granted, and tear everything apart until you are left with an undeniable truth.

Think of it as a way to reverse your thinking. You boil down everything to the most basic truth, rather than building an analogy that is just repeating what others think. First- principle reasoning will help you search for the truth because you question everything you know. Using an analogy, on the other hand, puts you in a position where you simply accept a widely agreed-upon truth, but is it really the truth? That is the question you need to be asking yourself.

If you don't learn to use first-principle reasoning, you will always be hooked on what people tell you is right or wrong, and you will always be trapped by others' assumptions. But when you do start stripping everything down, looking for the most basic and undisputed truths, you see the world for what it really is, not what others tell you it is.

Scenario Analysis

Scenario analysis is quite an important critical thinking approach, and it is one that plays a significant role in the world of investment. This is basically an approach to predicting future events by taking all possible outcomes into consideration.

This opens new doors for us because there are not only those alternative outcomes out there but also the paths that lead to them. Scenario analysis isn't based on past results or analysis of former trends; it doesn't stem from historical inputs or market indicators, which really forces you to think outside the box.

To practice scenario analysis, you need to think of the best, worst, and most likely outcomes to a scenario, but you need to act as if all are plausible and all are likely to happen. Generally speaking, it is recommended that you keep your scenarios down to just three, and you need to think of all three as "likely to happen". Once you manage to apply this principle to whatever discipline you want, it becomes highly unlikely that an unforeseen event will surprise you.

Chapter Four: Do It Like Socrates; Questioning to Think Critically

This entire chapter is dedicated to the Socratic questioning technique, which is one of the most important approaches to critical thinking. Socrates was a Greek philosopher and teacher, and he used this technique to get answers from his students while expanding their perspectives. According to Plato, one of Socrates's most renowned and gifted pupils, the latter believed that "the disciplined practice of thoughtful questioning enables the scholar/student to examine ideas and be able to determine the validity of those ideas."

In simple terms, Socratic questioning seeks to unravel truths and understand the meanings and motives through asking deep, pointed questions. It is a way of analyzing assumptions and concepts, distinguishing truths from half-truths, and what we know from what we don't know. Questioning is the technique on which all free thought is based. We are often told not to ask questions, and just to accept blindly certain things we're told. Socrates never settled for that, and he questioned everything so he could get to the bottom of things on his own. This is why Socrates is considered to be one of the greatest teachers of all time; to this day, Socratic questioning is used by teachers around the world who want to help their students understand what they really know as opposed to what they *think* they know. There is no better approach to probe a person's thinking and understand how they form their beliefs and ideologies, which is why Socratic questioning is also heavily used by lawyers as well as engineers and scientists. These are all people who want to find the truth and answer important questions.

So, how can you practice Socratic questioning? Well, you ask questions! The catch is in asking the right questions at the right time. Here is how you can do that.

Clarification/Understanding the Idea

The first set of questions in Socratic questioning pertains to clarifying the presented point of view. You use these questions to get the person to explain their point of view so you can explore the origins of their mindset and how they think.

What do you mean by ...?

Why do you say that?

Could you rephrase this or put it in another way?

Can you provide examples to explain your point of view?

How is this relevant to this discussion?

As you can see, these are all questions meant to elicit logical answers from the person you're talking to. This is not a way to try and corner the person and prove your point of view, but rather questions to help you really understand where they are coming from so you could form a clear idea on the origins of their thoughts and how they came to these conclusions.

Probing the Assumption

Now that you understand the person's idea clearly and have a solid grasp of what they mean by it, it is time to probe that assumption and challenge the person's beliefs. Again, this is not supposed to be a competition, but rather a way to help the person question their beliefs and rethink the foundations on which they base their arguments. This is a very important step in Socratic questioning because it is how you show people that there might be another way and that their approach here might not necessarily be right.

Why do you think this assumption is the right one?

What else could we assume here?

Is that always the case, or might things be different for one reason or the other?

Why/how did you choose those assumptions?

What happens if ...?

Why are you ignoring ...?

Why did you just focus on ...?

These questions are obviously intended to really probe the person's assumption and get to the root of it. This is how you get anyone to really rethink what they know and what they don't know. As explained earlier in the book, a lot of what we believe is just things we're told, and we rarely stop to think about them. Whether it is because of society, religion, or other influences, there is much that we take for granted without analyzing the truth behind those assumptions or beliefs. This set of Socratic questions will help you understand whether or not your beliefs are based on solid understanding and rational reasoning or are merely the result of cultural influences.

Probing the Reasoning

After the last set of questions, which was meant to dig deeper into the assumption and its roots, the person will provide evidence or rationale for how they formed such assumptions. This next batch of questions is aimed at extracting that reasoning or evidence. You shouldn't just take it for granted and assume that such reasoning is true. Socratic questioning means doubting everything and approaching the breaking down of each point as if it were untrue. And these questions will help you do that.

What makes you say that?

Why do you think this evidence make sense?

Is there a reason to question this evidence?

What do you think caused this to happen, and why?

How do you know that?

Is that enough reason to believe this assumption holds?

Why does that happen?

What would change your mind and prove this evidence doesn't make sense?

Do you have further evidence to support that claim? Do you need further evidence to support it?

Who says ... has to be true? By whose authority do we take this to be correct?

This set of questions is definitely some of the hardest to go through for the person on the other end (which could sometimes be you). This is because those questions force you to think of an explanation or reasoning for your reasoning! They also force you to rethink the validity of your claims. Who says that your evidence is adequate, or is even true in the first place? It is questions like these that really begin to expand the person's horizons and force them to realize that there might just be a different reason, and our own explanations don't always have to be right.

Exploring Different Perspectives

Now that you have the other person thinking, and questioning the validity of their reasoning, it is time to ask questions to offer and explore alternatives. There is always a different viewpoint and perspective, and the upcoming questions will help you, together, go through them.

What is the alternative?

Provide a counterargument to your own point of view.

How can you look at it from a different perspective?

Why is ... necessary, and can you think of another way?

Why does this make more sense than that?

Does anyone see it in a different way?

Who benefits from this?

What would ... think about this?

Why not compare ... and ...?

These questions will help the person begin to contemplate alternatives as viable options, which is a very crucial aspect of critical thinking. The more you make them think about the alternatives, the better the thought process they will have. They might still maintain their beliefs and assumptions after those questions, but they will do so after going through different possibilities and exploring the alternatives, which makes for a much healthier belief system and a more reasonable person.

Going Through the Ramifications and Implications

Next comes the process of exploring the consequences and implications of the assumptions. You need the person to start realizing that their assumptions and beliefs have ramifications, because maybe those ramifications will change their minds when put under the spotlight.

What effect would this have on ...?

How does this affect the outcome?

What are the consequences or outcomes of this assumption?

What are you implying by thinking this way?

What happens next?

How does this outcome fit into what you've already learned/known?

Exploring and probing the consequences might be one of the most important pillars of Socratic questioning and critical thinking. This is simply because the truth often lies in the eventual conclusion of our assumptions.

Probing the Questions

Now that you have gone through the assumptions, evidence, and consequences, it is time to question the questions that you asked so the person could see how this thought process worked overall.

Why do you think I asked that?

What was the importance of this question?

What does this question mean?

What else could I or should I have asked?

Which of these questions were most useful?

How can you use those questions in the future?

Socratic questioning will always be important to critical thinking, because the latter is about refining the thought process and finding the truth, and there's no better way to do that than asking the right questions at the right time. Socrates believed in the importance of questioning everything and accepting the limitations of our human knowledge.

Chapter Five: 9 Daily Habits to Prompt Critical Thinking

So, this all sounds quite good in theory, but how does it fare in practice? How exactly does one practice critical thinking? And is the use of those techniques feasible in our daily lives? They most definitely are, but that is not to say that it is easy to implement them. As we mentioned earlier in the book, critical thinking requires a great deal of restraint. It is in our innate human nature to want to rush things and pass judgments without really thinking things through. But for the many reasons mentioned on the importance and benefits of critical thinking, you will need to change that, and that is far from simple.

Still, with practice and discipline, you can become a critical thinker. But you need to start understanding and applying some principles in your daily life to prompt your mind and soul to implement critical thinking techniques. These daily habits will help you do so.

1. Worry About Finding the Truth Rather Than Being Right

This is possibly one of the most difficult habits to practice when it comes to critical thinking. We are often too blinded by pride and ego; people don't like it when they are wrong, and we want to have all the answers. If you put your ego aside for a moment, you will begin to see that you don't need to have all the answers, and it is fine to be wrong at times. Nobody is perfect, and your knowledge, vast as it may be, is quite limited in view of the overall scheme of things.

This is why it is important to start realizing that finding the right answer is much more important than being right. You should want to find the truth, not prove that it was you who got it. This mindset is key to becoming a critical thinker, and once you start practicing it, your life will change for the better.

At work, for instance, if a colleague or a subordinate suggests an answer to a problem, don't turn it down because it was better than yours. Work and ask questions to see if it was truly a better option. This will make you a better leader and more respectable human being. Much can be achieved if we put aside our egos and concern ourselves with only finding the truth.

2. Be Open to Differences

There are so many differences between us as human beings, and it can be easy to dwell on those and think of them as reasons to separate people. But critical thinking allows you to accept and embrace those differences. Learn to be accepting of varying ideologies and beliefs, and even embrace them. It is through these opposing viewpoints and beliefs that we can either reaffirm or change our own, and in turn, grow as people.

This kind of flexibility will help you think about different possibilities before rejecting them just because they are different. In the business world, this is a very important quality. Whether you are a leader or a regular employee, being able to accept different ideologies and approaches means you will get to explore all possibilities; no idea is off the table just because it comes from somewhere unusual. You will entertain all suggestions, and this will help you find better solutions and grow both personally and professionally.

3. Ask the Right Questions

The last chapter was entirely devoted to the Socratic questioning approach, which is indeed important to finding truths and meaning. But is every problem really that complicated that it warrants such an intense and rigorous line of questioning? True, a critical thinker is inquisitive and is always asking questions, but it is crucial that you ask the right ones. It happens quite often that you get too deep with your approach and complicate the analysis beyond its potential returns, and the original problem gets lost in translation.

You need to identify which problems require in-depth techniques like Socrates', and which could be adequately covered by asking basic questions; keep Occam's razor in mind, which states that the obvious answer is often the correct one. So, make your questions basic and to the point, and don't complicate things more than you need to. If you have a problem at work, ask questions like "What do we know so far?" or "How did that happen?" You should also ask, "What are we missing here?" and "How can we solve this?" It is questions like these that will keep you on point and help you get to the root of the problem and, in turn, find the answer, which might be very simple.

4. Stay Well Informed

This is one of the most important habits to promote critical thinking, and it is one that you should practice daily. Well-read people understand that there are different ways to look at a problem, and they are constantly exposed to varying viewpoints and perspectives. This helps them think critically of all possible angles whenever they face a situation that needs resolving.

Being inquisitive is key to critical thinking, which means that you need to keep up with what's happening around you in the world. Try to make a consistent effort to educate yourself on a variety of topics, whether they are related to your line of work or not; rest assured, anything you read or learn will come in handy one way or another in the future. The input you get on a regular basis gets stored in your mind, and it will be processed and utilized whenever needed. This will help you make better decisions in the future because you've gathered knowledge from a variety of sources and on a wide range of topics.

In short, dedicate a portion of your day to inform yourself on as many things as possible. Check the world news daily. Maybe you are into visual media, and in that case, make it a habit to watch an hour or so of a documentary every day. Needless to say, reading is essential, and it is a habit you must practice regularly because it will expand your horizons like nothing else. Reading helps you understand that there are different worlds out there, and that there are various angles and lenses from which you can view those worlds.

5. Develop Self-Awareness

Now, this is where things get really tricky. Our minds work at speeds we cannot even begin to fathom, and it is easy to make snap judgments or form opinions in a matter of seconds. You can't help it; your mind works in an automated mode with vicious speeds. Therefore it is crucial that you develop self-awareness and start trying to take control of your thought process. Your brain wants to reach the easy answer, and it wants to do it quite fast. But you are in control of your brain, and this means you can pause for a minute and reevaluate the conclusion you so quickly reached.

We all have our own biases and ideologies, and they can often get the best of us. But if you want to practice critical thinking, you need to be in control of your own thought process and personal biases. This begins by understanding those biases in the first place, because having an awareness of the prejudices you have towards certain ideas or sources of ideas is how you start combating those prejudices and thinking critically.

6. Be Organized

Yes, being organized in your life is crucial to critical thinking. Why? Well, critical thinking is all about organizing your thoughts rationally and viewing all given data in a clear manner. How can you expect that to happen if you can't even make up your bed or organize your desk at work? Always try to be organized when it comes to your surroundings, which will help you become more organized in your own head. Prioritize tasks; write your ideas on to-do lists, which is a great way to create mental space for other endeavors.

More importantly, you need to set goals. But you should be careful, though, as setting goals can be limiting at times. This is why it is even more important to develop a process or a system, because your goals are the finish line. But the system is something you can develop and improve as you work towards that finish line.

7. Be Your Own Critic

This is not to say criticize your actions or behaviors, but you need to be extremely critical of your thoughts. All the critical thinkers over the course of history continuously challenged themselves and repeatedly tried to find fault in their own reasoning. This is what you need to do so you can become more concerned with truths and meaning. Debate with yourself and go through arguments in your own head so you can begin to examine whether or not the reasoning behind your assumptions is valid.

8. Write

You'd be surprised how much different your thoughts would seem if you put them to paper. Writing is a basic form of critical thinking because it helps you flesh out your ideas and then strip them to readable, meaningful points -- when you get the hang of it, at least. If you want to get better at critical thinking, learn to write out your ideas and beliefs. You will find that writing helps you make a distinction between what you know (and can argue confidently) and what you *think* you know.

9. Seek Exposure

Critical thinking isn't exactly taught at most schools; in truth, it is generally rather frowned upon. So, how exactly do people become critical thinkers? Through exposure. We are the outcome of our collective experiences, and critical thinkers seek all sorts of experiences to help them develop their thought processes and grow as people.

We talked earlier about the importance of staying well informed and gaining exposure through the internet or books, but that isn't the only way to expose yourself to the world. You also need to meet new people, and the more different they are from you, the better. Engage in social activities and find people that challenge your beliefs and thoughts. They will make you a better person and an effective critical thinker. Critical thinking isn't exactly a skill you acquire, but it is something you learn and try to practice as much as you can. And seeking exposure however you can -through books, movies, documentaries, and/or meeting new people- will help you develop that tendency towards critical thinking.

Chapter Six: Avoiding Uncritical Thinking

Practicing critical thinking habits is only half the equation; the other half is trying to avoid uncritical thinking. There are quite a few things that you will need to do if you want to avoid uncritical thinking; read on to find the secrets to avoiding uncritical thinking.

Never Jump to Conclusions

This is possibly one of the hardest things to avoid because, as mentioned earlier, we humans like to pass judgments and jump to conclusions. Doing so means you completely skipped critical thinking for the easy way out (forming an uninformed and probably invalid opinion without taking enough time to consider your assumptions).

It happens quite often that when a person makes a claim you immediately jump to the conclusion that they are idiots and their claim is false, when in fact, if you hold off on the conclusions and consider their claim from different angles, it might actually start to make sense to you. This is obviously not an easy thing to do, especially when it comes to challenging your beliefs or ideologies you wouldn't want to change. But this is what critical thinking is about; you will learn so much and be receptive to so much more once you postpone jumping to conclusions until you have all the data and have considered it with care.

Keep Your Emotions Out of It

Ok, this is definitely harder than the previous one. Humans are passionate creatures, for the most part, and trying to keep our emotions out of an argument can be really difficult. Emotions are great, but they impair your judgment and hinder your critical thinking process.

If the subject matter was something dear and personal to you, say, your religion, then you could easily find yourself going down a slippery slope of emotion-based reactions. No matter how sensitive the topic is to you, learn to look at the face value of the presented assumption or claims. Never take them personally, because they rarely are. A person presenting an argument against your religion isn't necessarily attacking you, and you shouldn't get offended by it. Instead, take their claim, think it over from all possible angles, and then try to present your own theory or assumptions backed by evidence and logic rather than anger and bitterness.

Don't Linger in Your Comfort Zone

Let's face it, we all love our comfort zones, and why wouldn't we? Change isn't something humans are accustomed to or passionate about. There is a certain serenity and peacefulness about the mundane routine and repetition of our daily lives. Sadly, not much good can happen in terms of improving your thought processes, within the limitations of your comfort zone.

We are conditioned from a young age to accept certain facts and never to question them. We grow up, and a lot of those facts become our comfort zone. We don't dare challenge them as it would mean changing the status quo. The best example of uncritical thinking is lingering in your comfort zone and never second-guessing anything because it is just so easy to take things as they appear rather than trying to find truths and hidden meanings.

This is why you find a lot of people get quite defensive when a person challenges their belief system, whether that is pertaining to religion, society, or right and wrong in general. They don't want their realities shaken, and they don't want to be forced out of their comfort zones. If you are reading this, then you want to come out of your comfort zone, and you want to avoid uncritical thinking. This begins by challenging yourself and questioning everything you know, which is quite uncomfortable and will definitely leave you uneasy. But it is also your path to critical thinking and finding truths.

Avoid Over-Analysis

Believe it or not, overanalyzing things is one of the most popular uncritical thinking pitfalls a lot of people find themselves in without even knowing it. We have talked about the importance of critical thinking and how you need to question everything and analyze all angles. But sometimes, less is more. There are times when you over-analyze things, and you end up clouding your own judgment and creating assumptions where there shouldn't be any. This eventually leads to "analysis paralysis" in the decision-making process, and you end up worse off than you were before you tried critical thinking.

It is important to know when to stop analyzing. Look at the big picture and the details, because either or both have the answer that you're looking for. Accept the fact that you will never have all the information, which is okay. You can and should make a decision or reach a conclusion with what you have after applying critical thinking. But don't get so engrossed in your own thought process that you eventually get lost.

Embrace Your Individuality

One of the biggest manifestations of uncritical thinking is something we come across on a daily basis, which is group thinking.

A lot of people never take the time to think for themselves; they just follow the crowd. They find what the general consensus is, what most people believe to be right, and they adopt that point of view as their own, without ever thinking twice.

It is not really easy being different and adopting opposing viewpoints to what is considered the norm all around you. It takes effort and a lot of courage. Some people don't want to go through such struggles, so they just follow the majority to avoid confrontations. There are definitely those who follow mob mentality out of laziness, preferring to join the masses rather than formulate an opinion of their own.

In any case, mob mentality or group thinking is something you have to avoid. Critical thinking means questioning everything and debating all assumptions. Maybe you will reach an eventual conclusion that coincides with that of the majority, which is fine. But in that case, you will have reached it through conviction and by asking the right questions. In other words, you reached that conclusion on your own due to critical thinking, not because you wanted to take the easy way out.

Learn to embrace your individuality. It is okay to be different, and it is fine to not always agree with people. You have a brain; use it. The easiest path to uncritical thinking is being lazy with your thought process and following the masses just because you want the simpler solution, but that will not get you far in life, and you will probably always feel like something is missing.

Control Reflexive and Wishful Thoughts

Reflexive thinking is as the name would imply, something that you do instinctively, as a reflex, without consciously thinking about it. The core of critical thinking is thorough consideration and careful examination of assumptions and arguments; this is why it is very important to avoid reflexive thinking. You also need to make sure the questions asked are the right ones in the first place. It happens quite often that the wrong questions are asked, and they don't lead to where the problem lies.

Last but not least, you also have to avoid wishful thinking, because not only is it unrealistic, but it is also uncritical. We all have dreams and aspirations, but wishful thinking isn't based on facts or evidence. The outcome will not come true because of your faith, but it can come true because of certain evident facts. Faith is important in people's lives, but it cannot be blind faith, because that entails uncritical thinking and believing things without consideration of the facts. This is why you have to avoid wishful thinking at all costs.

SECTION 1: PROBLEM-SOLVING AND DECISION-MAKING

Chapter Seven: Why is Problem-Solving So Hard?

Why do we often have a hard time trying to solve problems we encounter on a daily basis? The reason is probably because you are not properly approaching the matter at hand. This happens without you even realizing it, mostly because we're programmed to deal with situations in a certain way that often prove to be incorrect or inefficient.

In this day and age, problem-solving skills aren't exactly a luxury or something you could do without. They are a must for any professional in the business world, and for any person really, because who doesn't encounter problems in their daily lives?

Before we get into how to solve problems properly, you need to know why you find it so hard to do so.

Focusing on the Bigger Picture

You keep hearing people say, "Focus on the big picture, that is all that counts", but that is not always necessarily the case. Sometimes, it is much more important to focus on the details and understand how they work, because the answer often lies within those intricate details. One of the most common reasons why a lot of people find problem-solving so hard is because they focus on the big picture only rather than trying to pay attention to the details.

Yes, the high-level view is important, and you will need it, but you also need to know when it's right to focus on the details because the answer to your dilemma might be there. For instance, a very common mistake a lot of people make is never reading the terms and conditions of a contract, such as a loan, for instance. They only see the bigger view, getting money to solve a financial pickle they're in. But the details of that loan might get you into even more trouble, which means not only didn't you fix your initial problem, but you also made it worse. This is a clear example of why the fine print matters. A lot of people fail to realize that, and they end up aggravating whatever problem they're facing instead of solving it.

If, however, you are a person who practices critical thinking, you already understand the importance of the details, and won't make a decision or come up with a solution without having all the data. A critical thinker wouldn't sign off on loans without reading the terms and conditions, as they realize that they have to cover all angles before committing to a solution.

Misinformation

Another very prevalent reason a lot of people have a hard time-solving problem is that they are misinformed or are missing information. Whenever you approach a certain problem, it is important that you have all your facts straight. You need all the relevant data, and that is the only way you will be able to find a proper answer or make an efficacious decision. Faulty or missing data can and probably will lead to faulty or incomplete solutions. A person who stays well-informed will keep up with news, updates, and relevant information before trying to handle any problem, so they will probably be able to identify faulty information and avoid using it. They would also be able to tell if there is missing information, and they'd hold off on making a decision until they have all their facts straight. This is why successful people never stop learning and are constantly trying to stay ahead of the game by reading and focusing on being well informed.

Ego

Too often, the reason why we can't solve a problem is that we can't even understand it. Inadequate phrasing and cryptic jargon can be quite difficult to decipher at times. How often have you attended business meetings where your managers used words you didn't understand, but you didn't ask because you were afraid you would look stupid or get scolded for it? This happens to the best of us, and it's because of our egos. If you can't comprehend what the problem is, how can you possibly hope to solve it? Problem-solving becomes ten times as complicated when you let your ego get the better of you.

This is why we focused earlier on in the book on the importance of putting your ego aside when seeking knowledge. A critical thinker would never let a poorly presented piece of information slide by in a meeting; they would stop the presenter and ask questions. They will keep probing until they are certain they fully understand the problem, which is why they will be able to solve it. A person who is too proud to ask, on the other hand, will leave such a meeting without having all the facts, which means they will not be able to solve the problem properly and they will get stuck, sooner or later.

Making Assumptions

People often make assumptions about the problem and its solutions before they even stop to consider it. When you critically approach a situation, you will stop to consider it from all angles, and you will think it through before making any assumptions. This increases the likelihood of you finding an answer to your problem, whereas assumptions will probably lead you down a dead end. Many let their preconceived notions and beliefs get in the way, stopping them from reaching a proper solution to the challenges they are facing.

Mindset

Too often, the biggest obstacle to problem-solving is the person's own mindset. The person, out of laziness, burnout, or some other reason, doesn't want to exert any effort to try and find a proper solution to the problem they're facing. This again brings us back to the importance of critical thinking, which ignites a passion to always seek the truth and to always try to find an answer. People who practice critical thinking understand that any problem can be solved, and everything has a possible explanation.

Another mental barrier that stops a lot of people from solving problems is their tendency to try past solutions that have been already tried by others. They rarely try to think of alternatives, no matter how obvious. Practicing critical thinking forces you to always consider alternatives, and there are even certain mental models where you have to take assumptions or alternatives into consideration no matter how absurd or meaningless they sound. This kind of flexibility is crucial to problem-solving; the fact that you are so set in your ways that you rarely stop to consider alternatives might very well be your problem.

Fear of Failure

Fear of failing is another reason why a lot of people find it difficult to solve problems. You start creating mental barriers that can stop you from finding an answer to whatever it is you are facing. This is a symptom of a bigger issue here, which is believing that failure is bad, and it is the end of the world; it is not. In fact, failure can be one of the best mentors out there. If and when you do start understanding that failing at something is an incentive and a way so you could learn, you will be able to analyze the reasons why that happened and learn something new, and you will try again. If you fail yet another time, you will learn something new, and so on.

There is a reason why all great inventors and scientists over the course of history were critical thinkers: that was the only way they could learn from their failures and grow. Thomas Edison failed thousands of times before finally inventing the light bulb, but he didn't view it that way; he said, "I have not failed. I've just found 10,000 ways that won't work." Once you start embracing your failures, you will find that they can help you a lot more than success can. You will put your ego and your irrational fears aside and seize whatever opportunities you have to try, no matter what the outcome is.

Problem-solving requires that kind of courage –the willingness to try different things out and not being thwarted by negative outcomes. Once you start having that belief and core understanding, it will be extremely hard to find a problem in your life that is too hard to solve, because you will be willing to do whatever it takes.

Chapter Eight: 6 Steps to Solving ANY Problem

Now that you know what the common obstacles are and why people often struggle with problem-solving, next, you need to create a system for yourself to approach problems you might encounter. This chapter is mostly focused on the steps that you should follow rather than tips to improve your problem-solving skills, which will be covered in the following chapter.

It is important that you become methodical and thorough with your approach to problem-solving because this ensures that you will be successful without encountering any of the problems we have mentioned in the previous chapter. Read on to find out just how you should approach the challenges you regularly encounter.

The Secrets to Problem Solving

1. Identifying the Problem

You will find that this is the first and most important step in your problem-solving endeavors, and all articles and videos on this matter will probably start with this one, for a good reason. How can you solve a problem that you cannot properly identify? This might seem like an easy thing to do, but it can be trickier than it seems.

It happens quite often that we get caught up in the symptoms or even solutions to the problem without focusing on the real issue.

This can be a slippery slope as you're simply taking your eye off the ball and shifting your attention to byproducts that will most likely not help you come to a proper conclusion. If and when you do identify the problem, you can get to the underlying causes and work on them, rather than just treat the symptoms.

So, in a nutshell, you need to identify the problem... but how can you do that? Start by asking the right questions, such as "Why is this happening?" You keep checking symptom by symptom and ask why that is happening until you can finally reach a point where you cannot explain why this is happening, which is the underlying root cause for the problem. This technique works for simpler problems with just a few consequences that can be targeted and carefully inspected, but for more complex matters you might have to up your game a bit.

When there are several symptoms and issues at hand, it can be rather challenging to pinpoint what the original problem is so you can work on it. The best approach to go about such complex matters is creating a visual representation of the problem at hand, which will help you envision a clear path to the root cause. You can create a concept map with all the key elements of the problem and how they are connected together, and it helps you trace back your steps to the main source of the issue at hand. Affinity diagrams are also very effective in breaking down bigger, entangled ideas into smaller chunks that can be properly managed.

2. Identifying Needs and Interests

You will find that many problem-solving models are weak this particular point, despite it being one of the more relevant ones. Any problem could have multiple solutions, but not all those solutions will cater to the involved parties' interests and needs, which is you need to take into consideration.

As we have mentioned several times earlier in the book, critical thinking prompts and encourages the consideration of any situation from all angles, and if you utilize it in problem-solving, you will come to see the importance of identifying people's needs when reaching a final solution. People's needs or interests won't simply be satisfied by just any solution, and the best answer is one that caters to everyone's needs and is satisfactory to all parties involved. So, whenever you approach a problem that needs solving, make sure to listen to what the involved parties have to say.

3. Analysis

You now have identified the problem(s), and the interested parties' needs pertaining to this particular matter; now you need to go into deep analysis mode so you can lay down possible solutions in the next step. Contrary to popular belief, identifying the problem and its symptoms is not synonymous with analyzing it. There is still much to be done before you can move on to the next step.

You need first to ask yourself if the problem at hand can be further broken down; this will often help you see it in a different light. Can you break it down to smaller issues or secondary problems that can be handled first? This compartmentalization of issues will make it significantly easier to solve the bigger one(s).

It then helps to try and look at the problem at hand from a different perspective. Is it possible that this isn't a problem if seen from a different angle? Different people might have different definitions as to what constitutes an issue and solving one for a person might complicate things for others. So, is this really a problem that needs solving? Are there people who don't view it as such? And if so, why don't they view it as an issue? Any concerns about the validity of the situation at hand need to be checked to avoid going about this the wrong way.

Critical thinking is your best tool in this particular step of problem-solving, as it will help you carefully consider all options and view the issue from all angles; it will also help you slow down and not rush into any conclusions which might turn out to have been a waste of time.

4. Exploring the Alternatives

When you reach this step, you should have all the input and data necessary to solve the problem, and it is time to start exploring the alternatives. In this step, you will try developing different solutions, and there will probably be quite a few. Those will directly be related to the causes which you identified earlier, which is why it is important that you follow the proper order while going about different issues, as your approach will still be the same.

When you have different solutions, you will need to start comparing them against one another to see which one yields the best results. Which answer will cater to the different interests, as explained in the second step? Will it maximize the reward based on your time and effort invested? Is this solution enough to completely take care of the problem? These are all questions that you will need to answer before selecting just one solution.

You can compare the pros and cons of each one to see which yields the best possible results, and you need to be thorough with this one. Again, critical thinking plays a huge role here, because you will need to put aside any biases or preconceived notions that you might have, to avoid confirmation bias. You don't want to find an answer that will prove you right or that conforms to your own beliefs; you want one that will solve the problem and ensure that all the involved parties are satisfied. So, be very careful with how you explore your alternatives and make sure you're extremely objective on this step.

5. Implementation

Next comes the implementation phase, in which you will take the solution you came up with and try to use it to solve the problem. It is important that you be quite thorough in this step, too, and you will need to carefully monitor progress so you could find out whether or not your solution was the right one.

It is also crucial here that you set goals that the solution should achieve, because how else will you measure progress and move on to the next step, called "assessment"? Your goals need to be very realistic. If your business, for instance, is suffering from a problem in its invoicing systems, your goals in fixing this shouldn't be generating 5 times as much revenue. It should be something more reasonable and measurable, like getting payments on time and getting more clients because of it. Experts always advise using the SMART method when it comes to setting goals: Specific, Measurable, Attainable/actionable, Relevant, and Time-bound.

When you use this technique, you will be able to set specific goals whose progress you can measure, because they are attainable and doable. They obviously have to be relevant to the problem at hand, and time-bound, since giving yourself no time limitations to see results is never a good idea.

6. Assessment

Assessing the efficiency of your solution is a must, and it is not exactly a luxury. The core of critical thinking believes that there are no absolute truths, and there aren't any easy solutions. Maybe your choice was not the right one, and you might need to find another. But how will you be able to do that unless you understand why the first solution didn't work? Assessment of your progress will help you do just that, and you will be able to identify whether or not the problem is indeed solved, and why it might not have been solved with your initial suggestion.

It is in this step that you will get back to the initial symptom or root problem to find out if it was resolved. If you find some symptoms or effects still in place, then you need to repeat your problem-solving process and come up with another alternative.

As you can see throughout this chapter, problem-solving isn't exactly complicated, but it isn't easy either. It requires precision and clarity, which is why critical thinking helps a lot when trying to solve any problems. You need that kind of meticulousness and inquisitiveness so you could get to the root of the issue at hand and come up with a proper solution.

Chapter Nine: 9 Problem-Solving Hacks to Learn

You now know the steps that you should follow when approaching any problem that needs solving. Sometimes, though, it is not just about the steps that you follow but rather how you implement them. The great thing about problems is the fact that they are unpredictable and different. Ok, maybe that's not so great. Still, that doesn't change the fact that your traditional approach to problem-solving might not work with each one you encounter. So, it is important to know some tips and hacks to help you tweak your approach whenever needed. These hacks will offer some great insights into how you can become a better problem solver.

1. Get Help!

Know the saying "two heads are better than one"? Well, it is true for just about everything, including problem-solving. You cannot always do it on your own, and sometimes it's best that you just get help. When you critically think about any problem you encounter, you will understand the importance of putting your ego aside so you can find a solution. As explained earlier in the book, there is nothing wrong with admitting that you don't have all the answers and that you might be misinformed at times. The important thing is having enough courage and self-awareness to take action based on that.

When you come to that conclusion, you will find it normal, and even preferable, to seek out people who can help you find a solution to the issue you have at hand. It is important to accept that there might just be people out there who have more knowledge about this particular situation than you and that they can help you see something that you might be missing. The answer often lies in plain sight, and having a second pair of eyes is always a good idea; it can help you deal with a lot of different problems that you weren't able to solve on your own.

2. Exercise Your Brain

Like all muscles in your body, your brain needs to exercise and stretch its analytical skills. Yes, a lot of problems have easy answers and can often be resolved with just a little effort. But a ton of others require creativity and thinking outside of the box. The latter is a term you have probably heard hundreds of times as an answer to all your problems. But how exactly does one "think outside the box"? Well, you need first to develop your analytical skills, or in other words, get your creative juices flowing.

A great way to do that is by playing puzzle and logic games, as well as others that require some mental effort on your side. Games like Sudoku or Rubik's cube help you work the problem backward, which is a great approach to finding a creative answer. Chess, on the other hand, is great for developing strategic planning skills, which will also help you think outside the box when trying to conquer a certain issue.

3. Take Your Time

It happens more often than not that trying to force an answer to the problem you are facing backfires. It is a lot like being in quicksand; if you keep kicking and trying to force yourself out as soon as possible, you will dig yourself deeper. If, however, you slow down and calmly approach your situation, you will begin to see the answer. The same can be applied to problem-solving. A lot of people want to find an answer as soon as possible, but it doesn't work like that. There is a lot of effort and thinking involved, which you cannot do if you're in a hurry.

This is why one of the most important hacks that you can follow to improve at problem-solving is slowing down. Take some time off from trying to find a way out, and carefully consider the situation you're in from all possible angles.

This also brings us back to the importance of critical thinking, as people who leverage it understand the importance of thoroughness and taking your time. They start early with trying to solve a problem, so they can take their time instead of being constantly in a hurry. It is crucial that you give yourself space and time to find an answer properly without rushing the process, because it is a process that takes time, and rushing it seldom yields positive results.

4. Sleep Well

Speaking of rest, sleeping well is actually one of the most important strategies for proper problem solving, or any success in life, if you think about it. You might not know it, but rapid eye movement (REM) sleep significantly enhances your brain's functions, and it can help you become much more creative. A study by Sara Mednick, Ph.D., assistant professor of psychiatry at UC San Diego and the VA San Diego Healthcare System, showed that "*REM sleep helps achieve such solutions by stimulating associative networks, allowing the brain to make new and useful associations between unrelated ideas*". The study also showed that these improvements are "*not due to selective memory enhancements,*" which often happen when we are awake.

In other words, getting a good night's sleep can make a huge difference in your cognitive and analytical abilities, so make sure you always rest and sleep well at night, especially when you have a challenging problem at hand.

5. Work Out

Believe it or not, it is not just your brain that you will need to exercise to develop your problem-solving skills. A lot of people don't seem to understand the importance of physical exercise, not just for their overall health, but also for their mental health. For starters, working out helps you relax, and this is a very important step towards problem-solving and mental acuity in general. This happens because your body releases several feel-good hormones, like endorphins, which elevate your mood when exerting physical effort.

We all know that exercising boosts cardiovascular health, but it also promotes mental health and could help you sleep a lot better, which, as mentioned earlier, is very important. Working out pumps more blood to your brain, which promotes new brain cell growth and preserves existing ones. In short, exercise can improve your mental health, and in turn, it can boost creativity and help you become a better problem-solver on many different levels.

6. Redo the Research

While explaining critical thinking and how we can leverage it, we mentioned the importance of being well-informed, and how that is one of the most important angles to critical thinking. When it comes to problem-solving, you obviously need to know all the factors affecting the situation. But maybe that knowledge isn't correct, or maybe you missed something on your first time around.

It is always a good idea to redo your initial research concerning the problem you are dealing with. It is quite possible that the reason why you can't find a proper answer is that you have the wrong piece of information, or a piece of the puzzle is missing. In that case, redoing the initial research to properly identify the problem and its root causes will do you a world of good. You cannot be lazy when it comes to problem-solving, because sometimes it is just a matter of going the extra mile to find the right answer.

7. Unplug

Sometimes, the answer to your problem lies in avoiding it for a while. Learn the importance of unplugging and the good it could do for your mental health. Go for a walk, read a book, watch a movie, meditate, talk to a friend, or do anything to take your mind off things. When you come back, you will be fresh and well-rested, with a new perspective that might just help you crack the problem. When you try too hard, and for too long, your brain often shuts down and finds it extremely difficult to handle the issue at hand.

This is why it is extremely important to have enough common sense and self-awareness to unplug whenever you reach a roadblock. The answer might be waiting around the corner when you come back with a fresh perspective that isn't tainted by exhaustion, mental fatigue, and stubbornness.

8. Use Different Senses

This might seem like an odd one, but utilizing different senses actually helps you with your problem-solving. For instance, instead of just squeezing your brain trying to come up with an answer, try saying the problem out loud! List the data you have and start conversing with yourself and asking logical questions, as you've learned earlier in the book. Sometimes, the answer to the problem needs just this kind of self-talk, because hearing the problem out loud can ignite the answer in your mind. If you can use your hands to engage in this particular problem solving, do it. Whatever senses you could leverage to find answers, use them.

9. Create a Mental Barrier

Believe it or not, often, the key to finding an answer to the problem you're facing lies in creating a psychological barrier in your head and distancing yourself from the said problem. Try to detach yourself from the situation at hand completely and think of the problem from another person's perspective. When you distance yourself mentally from the problem, you will start thinking more creatively because it is quite often the emotional or personal connection you have with the problem that is impairing your judgment and stopping you from finding a proper solution. When you kill that connection, temporarily, it becomes significantly easier to come up with creative solutions because you might be able to form unexpected connections between seemingly unrelated concepts.

Chapter Ten: Mental Errors that Make You SUCK at Decision-Making

Solving the problem is only part of the big picture, and compared to the next one, it might be easier. We are often faced with very tough decisions that need our attention, and we often fail at making the right decision. Just because you think you know the answer doesn't mean it is the right one. A lot of people find it extremely difficult to make decisions and for a good reason. It isn't easy. A lot usually hangs in the balance and knowing that makes things even more complicated.

Yet, it is not the ensuing consequences that make decision making this hard for most people. It is their own mindset that is often the obstacle that needs overcoming. You don't necessarily suck at decision making, but you are making some mental errors that are making it seem like you suck at this process. As explained earlier in the book, the first and most important step in solving a problem is identifying it. Read on to find out what mental errors are complicating the process of decision making for you.

Loss Aversion

This is one of the most common mental errors a lot of people make when it comes to decision making. We don't like losing; that is just a basic human quality. This fear of loss may cause us to make bad decisions at times. We don't want to lose what we already have, and that is a very effective way to stop yourself from gaining anything.

A business owner who has that fear will never move forward and take risks because they don't want to lose what they already have. This is the same as the person who would rather keep his year-end bonus in the bank than make a winning investment. We are simply programmed to protect the things that we already own, not necessarily because they are valuable, but because we don't want to lose them.

This can be a serious impairment for anyone, and it is something that is stopping you from reaching your full potential. So, to avoid loss aversion, take chances. Whenever you see an opportunity, stop thinking about what you already have, and start thinking about the rewards of this risk. Try to always look ahead rather than being short-sighted and focusing on the now. This is the only way you will be able to take risks and grow, not only as a professional or businessperson but also as a person. Much good often lies beyond the comfort zone of your current gains, and you need only to reach out to reap those rewards.

Overconfidence

Yes, too much confidence is a very bad thing, and it is a mental error that you have to avoid at all costs. There is a reason why even the most professional gamblers rarely have any money. Yes, they have mastered the game and are quite proficient, but they are way too confident in their own abilities, so they end up making very poor decisions.

The same can happen in the business world or in your personal life. You can be achieving considerable success and working steadily towards your goal, but if you get too cocky, you risk losing it all. You cannot think that highly of your own judgment because this means you are ruling out the possibility that you might be wrong. We discussed quite often in this book the importance of considering any situation from all angles and taking all factors into consideration before making a judgment. But overconfidence impairs all that, and it prompts you to make bad decisions because you think you know the answer, which isn't always the case.

As we also mentioned in this book, the ego can be a very dangerous thing, and you need to keep it in check, especially when it comes to decision making. Otherwise, you risk losing much because your mind left no room for debate. To avoid making poor choices due to overconfidence, you need to slow down and check all the details. Take a look at contradictory information that might be pointing to a different direction than the one you want to go with; never dismiss such information out of the belief that you have it figured out and that your data is already accurate.

More importantly, humble yourself. People make bad decisions every day because they never humble themselves, and they don't understand that they might be wrong at times. Embrace the fact that you might not know as much as you think you do, just like pretty much the entire human race. When you stop being overconfident and put aside your ego, more people will start contributing and offering alternatives, which you can then critically consider. Who knows, you might just find the right answer coming from someone else.

Anchoring

This is one of the most dangerous mental errors that we all make on a regular basis, mostly because we're led into this trap by companies and advertisers. Anchoring simply refers to how our minds are affected by the first impression, and how we anchor to those and make poor decisions based on that fact. This technique is usually leveraged by business owners to trap customers. For instance, you see fancy shoes all around storefronts in your city, each costing over $400. When you finally enter a store offering a pair for $250, you don't stop to consider the fact that these shoes are also way too expensive. This is because your mind is anchored by the higher prices you viewed, which makes it more open to buying something that is cheaper than the initial prices, but nonetheless overpriced.

A pizza store that limits the number of toppings you can add to 5 sells a lot more than one that doesn't have any limitations when it comes to toppings. This is again because our brains are anchored by the highest average we see, so we buy more, as long as we are within the range. Many of the high-end products of a certain business aren't really expected to sell, but they do help the company sell a lot of mid-range products by anchoring your mindset and making them seem much more affordable and appealing.

As you can see, this is a slippery slope, and it easily leads to poor decision making. You can't really avoid anchoring, because this is simply how our brains are wired, and we cannot do much about that. You can, however, minimize the effects of anchoring so you could make better decisions in the future. For starters, check multiple starting points or sources so you could have different takes on what the average truly is rather than just using the last source you checked as the foundation on which you will make your decision.

You also have to make sure you are more concerned with value rather than pricing. Try to look behind the face value of what you are offered and find a real and tangible return on your investment, whether it be time, money, or effort.

Sunk Cost Trap

This is another mental error that we often find ourselves making, and it is also born out of ego. Sunk cost trap is when you keep going through with a bad investment or idea because you have already invested time and money, so you keep pushing forward, hoping that the tide would turn, and the decision would yield good results. While that might make sense in certain cases, at first, you need to have enough sense and reason to know when to pull the plug.

We don't like to admit we were wrong, which brings us to the importance of critical thinking. It will help you put aside your ego and consider the situation from a neutral point of view. If the decision made is proving to be bad for business, then you will analyze the reasons behind that and try to undo that decision. This is what critical thinking is all about; logical, meticulous consideration of the facts, regardless of the implications. You need to start applying that to your professional and personal life, even if it means your ego would take a blow, because making sound decisions is a lot more important than your feelings.

You cannot afford to keep pouring money into an investment that isn't yielding any profits. This is why it is important that you critically think about the problem, which means removing yourself from the initial decision and not associating it with your own personality. It happened, and it's time to move on and figure out the best step forward. Ask others what their take is on the decision at hand, and whether or not they think it is a mistake that needs to be undone. More importantly, understand that it is fine to make mistakes and allow yourself to make them. What counts is not going through with the mistakes, and making better decisions in the future.

The Availability Heuristic

If you looked up the availability heuristic, you would find that it is defined as a mental shortcut, and it is one we are often guilty of making. This is when we assume that the first thing that comes to our minds when we think about a problem or decision is the most important point. The availability heuristic is when you assume that just because you remembered a thought, then it must be more important and relevant than any other counter argument or opposing thought.

For instance, if you asked a random person on the street if they think the world is doing well or not, they will most likely tell you it is not. People are getting poorer, and there is much poverty in the world right now. Reading so, you probably don't disagree. Well, believe it or not, poverty has gone down drastically over the past couple of centuries, and it is at its lowest rates ever right now. We simply assume the opposite. This is because we live in an age of information, and we are often faced with bad news -- because it sells better, and it also lingers in our brains a lot more. That doesn't necessarily mean that this is the truth, though, as proved by our last example. We tend to overestimate and put too much stock into the things we can remember and do the exact opposite with things we don't know or haven't heard.

People still refuse to believe in some of those facts because they are not aligned with what they hear on a regular basis and see on TV and in newspapers, which is why availability heuristic is dangerous and often leads to poor decision making. You need to leverage critical thinking, carefully consider any arguments you make, and base your reasoning on facts and evidence rather than the first piece of information that pops into your mind. This will help you slow down and understand that there might be a different truth out there than the one you think you know. And in turn, you will be able to make better decisions.

Chapter Eleven: How to Make a Tough Decision

So, now you know why you often fail at decision making, and the mental errors that make it such a challenging process for you. What comes next? Well, learning how to make those tough decisions that plague you at night, keeping you awake for long hours. But before we get into tips on decision-making, why is it do we often face a hard time making them, mental errors aside? You pause at a restaurant menu for half an hour, confused on what you should order. "Should I order them all?", you wonder. This hesitance, unfortunately, persists when it comes to bigger decisions at work and in our personal lives, which can be quite problematic. There are some very simple reasons why you feel this type of hesitance before making a decision.

One of the main reasons why decisions can feel so complex and tough at times is because we have this innate fear of missing out on the other choice. When you're at a restaurant, you're not sure what to get because you're worried that the choice you neglected might be better than what you're getting. If you're hiring new employees, choosing between two qualified candidates feels tough because you dread making the wrong choice.

Another reason we freeze when it is time to make a decision is dreading the consequences. It can be quite the debilitating feeling to feel the weight of responsibility resting on your shoulders, and as a result, people often get hung up on the outcomes and fail to act.

The Secrets to Making Tough Decisions with Ease

Getting the Facts Right

We have talked earlier about the importance of being well-informed, and it really shows when it comes to decision making. Critical thinking doesn't just focus on the importance of getting your facts right, but on the probability that when you have all the relevant information and facts, you will be able to make a tough decision properly because you are informed.

How can you fire an employee just based on your middle management's recommendation? You need to see their progress reports, inspect samples of their work yourself, and even have a sit-down with them to see if they are as bad as their direct managers say they are. How can you decide to buy a car out of your three possible options without meticulously reviewing each's specs and performance? It is this kind of thoroughness and attention to detail that will help you make informed decisions that lead to good results.

What Do You Believe In?

This is an important question you will need to ask yourself before making any tough decisions. Any choices stem from your own belief system and set of values, and it can be easy to lose sight of your own ideologies while struggling with a tough decision. So, always remind yourself and review your motives and values, because the answer to your dilemma often lies in reviewing your own beliefs.

Focus on a Single Feature

Also known as the "single-feature model", this is one of the best approaches that you could follow to make tough decisions. One of the biggest reasons why some decisions can be so hard is because of the fact that there are often too many options. The purpose of this model is to boil down the comparison between the various models into one single feature which you will use to make a final decision, which makes it exponentially easier.

For instance, using the previous example mentioned earlier, if you have two perfect candidates for a junior vacancy in your company, focus on a single feature and make it the deciding factor. It might be years of experience, for example. So, if candidate A has 2 years of experience and B has 3, then you will go with the latter based on this model.

You should know, though, that the single-feature model might not be ideal for more complex decisions, because you ignore several other variables in the equation and focus on just one, which won't always be wise. So, use this strategy for tough decisions that don't have major consequences, and when you're pressed for time. In other words, if that last example was about a director's position, then taking just experience into consideration wouldn't be wise.

Consider the Long Run

We might be envious of people who are quite capable of thinking on their feet, making quick decisions whenever needed. But that is not necessarily a good quality to seek. When it comes to decision making, it is important that you think long term, because the consequences of complex and tough decisions are often seen and felt in the long run.

Yes, it will feel terrifying once you start looking that far ahead and figuring out the consequences of your choice, but how else will you make a tough decision if you don't think of its outcome years down the line? As we've constantly mentioned in this book, one of the most important pillars of critical thinking is being able to analyze a situation from all angles, including a future one. We tend to make decisions quickly, and we are wired to respond as fast as we could. Sometimes that works; other times, it won't. Humans are reactive creatures by nature. We respond to our circumstances and have an urge to come up with a solution before thinking it through. If you want to really make tough decisions, you will have to learn to control that side of you.

Leverage critical thinking techniques and carefully consider the repercussions of the decision you're about to make. Keep your thoughts and emotions under control. This will help you think long term and take all angles into consideration, which will exponentially improve your decision-making skills.

Create a Routine

A very efficient strategy for improving your skills is trying to reduce decision-making fatigue. Trying to come up with the right decision all the time can be very draining, and it could lead to you making poor ones just because you want to get it over with. So, what do you do to avoid this problem? Well, you create a routine for those tough but regular decisions.

It can be something as simple as not being sure which route to take to work every day. Eliminate the decision-making; choose one fixed route that you will take every day no matter what. This makes your life a bit easier, and you will be able to channel that energy into more significant and complicated decisions. Can't decide what to have for lunch at work every day? Make a routine out of eating a fruit salad for lunch every day at work. These routines will help you expend less energy on making tough but rather unimportant decisions.

What if it is an unexpected situation or choice that you encounter? Can you make a routine out of such decisions? You actually can, in a way. Deciding on what to eat for lunch every day is easy, but what would you do if you find one of your employees slacking around at work all the time? Should you talk to them about it? Should you issue a warning letter? Should you fire them on the spot? This is the type of decision that you need to routinize so you could deal with such cases with relative ease and make the right choice every time.

Here, you can follow an "if" rule to streamline your decision making. Make an "if rule" for yourself, such as "If I come out of my office 3 days in a row at 2 p.m. to find an employee sleeping on his desk or talking to his co-worker, I will talk to them. If the same thing happens two days after that, I will issue a warning letter. If this persists for the entirety of the following week, I will terminate them". That way, you create a routine out of dealing with employees who don't take the job seriously. You will obviously critically think about the situation and come up with a proper response to each scenario, but once that is done, you will be ready to make quick, informed decisions without having to waste any time or energy. Routine is often frowned upon in life, but when it comes to decision making, it can really help you get some efficient results and maintain your sanity.

Get Other Opinions

This one won't be easy for many people, but it is quite relevant, nonetheless. Who said decision making has to be an individual struggle? Sure, when it comes to those tough decisions, you will eventually be the one who decides. But critically thinking about a problem or a tough choice means understanding that you might not have the right answer, and maybe someone else does. So, why not get opinions? Talk to others and get different insights. See what they have to say and which choices they prefer and why.

Maybe someone else's insights would broaden your horizons and bring something to your attention that you have been missing. It never hurts to get a second opinion, no matter how sure of yours you are, because there isn't just one right answer. And talking to people and getting their opinions might help you take that tough decision that has been troubling you.

A final tip to this decision-making dilemma is to set a timer. It happens quite often that you will face a lot of different choices, and each could be very lucrative or very costly. You go through them all and inspect all the possible angles, and they still remain attractive. This is why it is important to set a time limitation, because you cannot linger on such decisions for long, especially in the business world. There isn't necessarily one right answer, and you will never know it until you shed your fears and move forward.

Chapter Twelve: Pro Decision-Making: 5 Expert Secrets Revealed

Now you know the basics of decision making and how you can get it done with ease. But is it really as simple as that? Well, it probably isn't. You still will face some challenging times trying to come up with the right answer, and it will happen more often than you'd like to admit. This brings us to the next question; do all smart and successful people suffer as much as us regular folks when it comes to decision making?

They probably do, but they also have some tactics and secrets that could help them make the right choice, or at least not spend weeks worrying about it. Finding those secrets might be hard, but we have compiled a list of expert secrets that could really make decision-making much simpler for you.

Forward Thinking

This is not just an expert secret, but it is also a habit practiced by all successful people around the world. As an expert on high-performance leadership, Dr. Paul Schempp puts it thus: "Forward-thinkers look for solutions, but the backward-thinkers look for justifications." Reading this, your eyes are probably glowing. You know a lot of people like that, and you might even be one. In fact, we've all been there a lot of times.

You do backward thinking when a new iPhone is released, and you go buy it. You find justifications after making the purchase -my current phone is getting older, it won't get software updates, and so on. You do this as opposed to thinking forwardly and trying to find how this new iPhone will solve a problem for you. We do the same with important decisions in our life. You see managers firing employees because they had an argument. They then try to justify it by blaming it on the employee's behavior, rather than looking ahead and critically thinking whether or not that employee was an asset that should have been left to continue working.

As Dr. Schempp explains, great decision-makers take their time at first to identify the problem and look for solutions. This helps them make fast and efficient decisions once they have identified the problem and its root causes. In a nutshell, a backward decision-maker focuses on the symptoms. Instead of asking why the employee got stressed and raised their voice, you fire them because they stepped out of line. A forward decision-maker would ask the employee what's stressing them and why their behavior has changed. This, in turn, will help them make a proper decision on the situation that could actually work things out.

Leverage Your Core Values

Professor of decision-making, Dr. Joe Arvai, on the other hand, believes that the reason why a lot of people are incapable of good decision making is that we seldom think about the big picture. We dwell on the smaller points and subtext. He also sees that people fail to make the connection between the decision at hand and their own set of values and beliefs.

He believes that decisions are mirrors that reflect our beliefs and values, and as such, we need to make decisions based on those. "Decisions define who you are as a person," Dr. Arvai adds. He explains that by making your values a building block for your decisions, you will be able to determine your goals and objectives, come up with options to choose from, determine the consequences of your decision, and lastly, decide if there are any trade-offs. When you make everything relative to your values, decision making becomes exponentially easier, because every choice you make has a solid foundation and reasonable justification.

This brings us back once again to the importance of critical thinking, as it is the only way you will be able to determine your own values and beliefs. Questioning everything and learning to think critically about everything around you will help you determine a set of core values and beliefs. When you start inputting those into your decision making, tough decisions won't be so tough anymore.

Learn from Your Past Decisions

Believe it or not, one of the best secret weapons to better decision making is failing in some. But the ones you do fail at will teach you so much. We are programmed to fear failure, and it is often our worst enemy, but is it really? Self-development guru Tony Robbins advocates the importance of learning from your past decisions so you could make better ones in the future.

He emphasizes the importance of having contingency plans, so you avoid losing altogether. Everybody makes decisions, and not all will be the right ones. But successful people always have a backup plan to protect their investment, whether it be time, money, or effort.

When you have a safety net then nothing can go horribly wrong because of your decision, even if it does not go as expected. When you use your past decisions as mentors, you will be able to better prepare for future ones.

Balanced Knowledge

For the millionth time, we will talk for a minute about knowledge and the importance of knowing all the facts about a decision you are about to make. But can this backfire? Is there such a thing as knowing too much? Well, according to Mikael Krogerus & Roman Tschappeler in a very popular TEDx talk, yes, too much knowledge can translate to confusion and impair your judgment. In fact, these experts claim that if you compared the brain scan image of a person who knows too little and another who knows too much about a decision that needs to be made, they'd be the same. So, in other words, they are both equally confused and unable to make a meaningful decision.

This can be explained by the "choice overload" problem, where our brains can't decide because we are faced with too many options. Too much knowledge can put too many options on the table, and in turn, confuse you when you're trying to reach a decision. This is why Krogerus and Tschappeler recommend having enough knowledge to limit your options, whether that is with the Netflix film you're going to watch that night or with major life decisions. Once you feel like you have covered all your bases thoroughly, then you should make the decision.

Experts also explain the importance of not being a perfectionist when it comes to decision making. Learn to be satisfied. You cannot make the perfect decision, but you can make the best one possible within your abilities, and that is what you should strive to achieve rather than perfection. Was there a better option? Possibly. Could you have done any better? If you critically thought about the problem from all angles and did all the right things, then probably not. So, don't dwell on the idea of perfection and just make up your mind!

Trust Numbers, Not Gut Feelings

People tend to overestimate just how accurate their gut feelings are. You see this businessperson telling you it was their intuition that landed them the deal with a major client, and that gambler telling you it was their gut that won them the jackpot. Poker champion Liv

Boeree has a different take on this. She believes our gut feelings are great, but not for "everyday things that we have a ton of experience with." This applies to intuition, like knowing whether or not your loved one is angry without them saying so or getting a feeling that the roads are going to be crowded today.

She argues that logic and analysis -in other words, critical thinking- are much better suited for major life decisions. Switching jobs, choosing career paths, selecting spouses, and all those major decisions are better left to numbers-crunching and careful analysis. Boeree adds that our intuition is important, but when you're making a major decision, be meticulous and thorough. Don't trust your gut feelings, because they are never enough to make such important choices.

SECTION 2: BELIEFS, LOGICAL FALLACIES AND COGNITIVE BIASES

Chapter Thirteen: How Beliefs are Formed (And Influenced)

In the first chapter of this book, we discussed the brain's physiology and how the human mind works, but we never really answered the question of where thoughts come from. Why do we have different beliefs, and are hell-bent on trying to prove that ours is the right viewpoint? Why do some people believe in Christianity, while others choose Islam or Judaism? Better yet, how come certain people forego religion and god(s) altogether, becoming atheists or agnostics? These are all very important questions worth answering if you are to get an idea of how our beliefs are formed, but there isn't just one straight answer.

A person's beliefs are formed and influenced by a variety of factors, and they all eventually contribute to the collective awareness of the individual as they grow up. There are several sources from which a person's beliefs are formed, and we will go through them one by one in this chapter.

Sensory Perception

Before we get into the more philosophical side of things, the easiest way for a person to form a belief in something is through sensory perception. This is quite as simple as it sounds. We view and experience the world through our senses, which is why it makes sense for us to have certain ideas or beliefs imprinted in our heads based on those senses.

You know that fire is hot and hurts you because you've experienced it when you were playing with matches as a kid. That sensation is forever imprinted in your mind, and you will deal with fire accordingly. You know that the sun is too bright since you've tried looking at it once, and it hurt your eyes. This is what we mean by sensory perception, and it is something we all experience and develop as we grow older. Yet, critical thinking would have you question even your senses. What if you are hallucinating? What if the things you are experiencing aren't really real? This is why even when it comes to your own senses, the techniques explained in this book count.

Outside Circumstances

Whether we'd like to admit it or not, much of your beliefs are developed on a geographical basis. If you were born in Saudi Arabia, you would most likely be a Muslim rather than a Christian or a Jew. If you were born in Rome, chances are you will grow up to be a catholic. No matter how much people vehemently stand up for their belief system, much of it wasn't even their choice in the first place.

When a person is born, they are given a name, gender, and most likely a certain religion in many areas across the world. Then as you grow older, you start thinking and observing for yourself, and then your beliefs are formed in relation to the authority of wherever you are; religious doctrines and clergy, police, laws and regulations, and plenty of other forms of authority. If you grew up in a country where it is illegal and forbidden by law and religion to hold hands with your spouse on the street, chances are you will believe it is something extremely wrong and to be prohibited at all costs.

The "nature versus nurture" argument has been around for centuries. But regardless of where you stand on this debate, the fact of the matter is that wherever you are born, the existing circumstances in that place play a monumental role in forming your belief system and core values as you grow up. We take to those around us, which is probably the most important external circumstance responsible for shaping our beliefs as we grow older.

As an adult, you don't put as much stock in what others believe as you did when you were younger. But at that younger age, you are basically a sponge. You see what those adults around you do, and you take after them. You do as they do and believe as they believe. Therefore, we have repeatedly said throughout the book that critical thinking is something you must apply to your own core values. You need to start thinking for yourself and determine whether these are really things that you believe in, and not just doing/preaching them because this is what you grew up to find happening around you.

Personal Intuition

If and when you start to question and think critically about everything you have been taught, your beliefs will stem from a whole new place: yourself. You will no longer be just repeating what others have told you without understanding why and how. When you start asking, "Is this really true?" you will find that your entire mindset is changing and transforming into an inquisitive and skeptical version.

This doesn't happen overnight. But once it does, your personal intuition and gut feelings will form your belief system. The more you think critically about life and all things surrounding you, the better you will be able to form your values based on personal conviction rather than blind obedience.

Working on developing your own intuition and reasoning will lead you to utilize other tools to help you form and influence your beliefs. You will find causes and purposes for each of your value sets and personal ideologies. You may even ultimately return to your initial beliefs that you were raised to follow, but if that happens, they will be yours and no one else's.

Logic is a very important psychological factor that also influences all our beliefs. Critical thinking allows you to leverage logic and analysis to try and see things through a different lens, which will eventually change your perspective. It doesn't even have to be the big question, "Does God exist?" It could be something simpler, like changing your opinion on an employee's performance, regardless of how you personally feel about them. Seeing numbers and a track record of excellent performance helps you see that, and you will be able to use these observations to change your beliefs about that person. It is not easy, but it can make you open to change and differences, because logic is the wall against which all false arguments and empty rhetoric crumble.

Science

Some people form their beliefs based on science and science alone. They believe in hard evidence, and they have no need for assumptions, faith, or wishful thinking. Regardless of what you might think of this particular belief system, it is out there, and it does make sense. When a person bases their beliefs on just facts and data, they are only trusting what they can see, hear, or experiment with, and that is something to be respected.

The scientific method lets you see the world for what it really is, rather than what you want or need it to be. Is it ideal? For a person who has faith as their driving motive, no, it is not ideal. Still, this approach will help you find something very important: an unbiased answer. We may all come up with an answer or have an opinion/belief about something, but very few are able to produce an unbiased one. It is not easy to remove all personal biases and preconceptions while trying to examine a situation.

Yet, with the scientific method, which is deeply rooted in critical and analytical thinking, people are able to form unbiased beliefs that are based on the facts and the facts alone. "The numbers don't lie" is definitely not a bad foundation on which to build your beliefs.

Maintaining Equilibrium

Also known as homeostasis, this is simply our desire to maintain the status quo. Our bodies work to regularly maintain a regular heartbeat, breathing, temperature, and a host of other functions. Yet, your brain also works to maintain a state of homeostasis when it comes to your personal beliefs. This is why this condition is a driving factor behind many people's beliefs, and it is this quality that is responsible for triggering violent reactions and responses in many people.

They simply don't want to change that state of equilibrium, so they lash out if a person tries to influence that condition or, worse, shatter it. This state of cognitive stability is very tempting, and you can dwell on it all your life; most people do, as a matter of fact. Why is that? Well, simply because doing otherwise takes a lot of time and effort. Trying to change your core beliefs or perception of the world requires some serious brain activity and a lot of mental effort, which is not something most people do lightly. Our brains don't easily make such an investment of effort and time, which is why a lot of people simply maintain the status quo and avoid disrupting the existing cognitive homeostasis. They just stick to what they know rather than trying to disrupt the system. Needless to say, this is counterintuitive to everything we have been saying throughout the book.

Biases

Perhaps the most common way a person's beliefs and values are formed is through biases. We will get to talk a lot more in the upcoming chapters on cognitive biases and what they mean, but for now, let's just discuss the general idea. It is simply how we lean towards certain points and ideologies in favor of others. There are dozens of different biases, and they can all be misleading, anchor our judgment, and push us in one direction because it is the comfortable one rather than the correct one.

Some of these biases can be innate in our own nature, like overconfidence and being inclined to trust your own judgment more often than others'. In other cases, biases are learned and inherited from society and those around us, like pretty much any bias you see against color, creed, religion, or sex.

Chapter Fourteen: Logical Fallacies vs. Cognitive Biases

Picking up from the last chapter, in this one we will discuss the difference between cognitive biases and logical fallacies. Contrary to popular belief, they are not one and the same. They are both thinking errors, yes, but they stem from completely different roots, and the degree to which you can control both is completely different.

In simple terms, a logical fallacy is an error in logic; your way of approaching a certain argument or ideology is flawed by erroneous data. With some practice and experience, you can learn to avoid those lapses in judgment and how to think without falling into those logical fallacies. Cognitive biases, on the other hand, result from your mind's tendency to think in a certain way or the other. You can change your thinking approach by correcting fallacies, but biases are how you process information in the first place, and that makes it much harder to avoid them.

Cognitive biases are not necessarily errors in how you think; it's just how you tend to do it. As we mentioned, it is how your brain processes information and experiences, and this mechanism cannot exactly be altered just because you want to. In other words, biases aren't a bad thing per se, because they are the lens from which we view reality, but they might often be distorted. This is why it is crucial that you become aware of biases in your thinking, and when to allow them, as opposed to when you should try to critically think about a matter and offer a fair assessment in spite of your cognitive biases, which is exactly what it means to be a critical thinker.

That being said, spotting your own biases is very tricky, because your mind often shows you that your thinking is correct and the right way to go because of those biases. But we will get to that in a later chapter. For now, the first step to identifying and processing biases and fallacies is knowing the different ones out there.

Cognitive Biases

1. Liking/Loving Tendency Bias

This is one we are all guilty of at one point or another. Ever heard of some unexpected behavior committed by a famous athlete or celebrity you love? We often tend to excuse or overlook such incidents, because our brains instruct us to ignore the faults of the people we admire because of this like/love tendency bias. Those feelings of admiration and love for others can be very powerful, and, therefore, they often impair our judgment and mislead us.

2. Confirmation Bias

Confirmation bias is another very common one that you probably do quite often without even knowing it. This cognitive bias is our tendency to try and align the outcomes of research to our own beliefs. When you are working on something or trying to present an argument, you sometimes try to collect or recall information that supports your own hypotheses and beliefs. How many times have you been in an argument, and you just mentioned the facts that support your claim, purposefully or unintentionally overlooking other pieces that might contradict you? This doesn't mean you are a bad person; it is just that when we have an emotional attachment to the outcome, we tend to try and prove what we already believe in.

This also happens when you interpret vague and inexplicable evidence in a way that supports your belief. You've probably heard the whole "We don't know where the universe came from, so God must exist" argument more than once. The people presenting such an argument aren't necessarily zealots, but they just want to interpret the facts in a way that proves what they already think, because it is easier that way.

3. Disliking/Hating Tendency

This is the exact opposite of the first cognitive bias we mentioned. Just as liking someone could make you overlook their shortcomings, hating them can make you ignore their virtues. We might even be inclined to distort the facts to feed that hatred or dislike of a person or thing. Again, this doesn't imply that the person with this cognitive bias is bad or hateful, but humans are passionate creatures, and there are things and people that we simply dislike. The problem with this one is how it makes you even hate all things associated with the person or the concept which you oppose, so you end up wasting a lot of opportunities for critically thinking about it.

4. Automation Bias

Automation bias is exactly what the name implies. It is when you trust a machine's judgment more than yours, simply because we rely too much on technology and put too much stock in machines' abilities. Technology has changed our lives and helped us in a million ways, yes, but that is a double-edged sword. When you start trusting automated systems' judgment more than yours, problems arise, because at the end of the day those are still just machines, but your judgment and personal supervision is what counts.

People sometimes ignore blatant facts and contradictory information, just because automated systems say otherwise. This stems from automation bias, which makes us put too much faith in machines as opposed to humans.

5. Inconsistency Tendency

People don't like change; it is in our innate human nature. We like maintaining the status quo, and that often results in errors in judgment. This creates a cognitive bias where we are resistant to change and makes us reluctant to find a solution to get over our bad habits. This anti-change behavior makes it much more difficult for a person to change their ways and eliminate bad habits, which results in further complications in the future.

6. Attentional Bias

If there is another quality that most humans share, it is a short attention span. We are easily distracted, and our minds tend to recollect the nearest piece of information to solve the puzzle. Attentional bias is when your perception is affected by recurring thoughts at the time. This makes it much more difficult for you to think of alternatives, because your line of thought is already going in one direction, and you can't help but decide or present an argument affected by that line of thought.

To give an example: if, for the past couple of days, you were obsessed with your weight and read a lot about the dangers of obesity, you might be inclined to reject that application to a new vacancy at your company because the prospective employee was overweight. Your mind associated obesity with negative thoughts and emotions, and it affected your judgment and excluded other points from the equation.

7. Curiosity Tendency

We are very curious creatures. We always want to find out more about new things around us. While that can be considered a good quality since it drives us to explore the world around us, it can also be quite a dangerous tendency. This curiosity tendency pushes you to try things that might be bad for you, just because you want to know what it would be like. People who have never gambled or done drugs still hold some curiosity as to what it feels like to engage in such vices, and they may give it a go because of curiosity tendency.

8. Bandwagon Effect

Ever heard the term "jump on the bandwagon"? Well, that is actually a cognitive bias that we find ourselves drifting towards more often than not. It is when people tend to accept beliefs and ideologies simply because a large number of people do. As many agree on something, others "jump on the bandwagon" to join them in agreement. There are many reasons why people might be affected by this particular bias. Sometimes it is the person's own tendency to conform to what others around them believe, or a desire to fit in with society's norms. In other cases, a person is not well informed, so they derive their information from others and base their own judgment on the "facts" they received from third parties.

9. Kantian Fairness Tendency

The world is not a fair place, and that is something we all have to come to terms with sooner or later. Unfortunately, a lot of people cannot do that, and their mind is always affected by this cognitive bias. They tend to be fair and show kindness when they shouldn't. In other words, they act ideally and as best as they can because they think this would be reciprocated in the future. Needless to say, that doesn't happen, and those people end up suffering for it. Picture standing in a very long line at the DMV, when a person cuts in front of you, saying they have an emergency to which they need to attend. People with a Kantian fairness tendency will allow that to happen, often even if a second and a third person come and ask to cut in line. They showed what many would construe to be weakness, but it is rather a misplaced idealism.

10. Compassion Fade

This cognitive bias is when we feel a lot more compassion towards a small number of victims that can be identified rather than a much larger group of anonymous ones. There is this quote that is often incorrectly attributed to Stalin: "The death of one man is a tragedy; the death of millions is a statistic." This is pretty accurate, and it is how we process the news we get hit with on a daily basis. You feel some sadness when you hear about a soccer player who died alone on a private plane crash (even if you are not a fan of the sport), more than you do when you hear about an entire commercial plane crash where 200 people died.

11. Reciprocation Tendency

Remember that time your friend got you an unexpected gift for Christmas? You suddenly feel the urge to get them a gift in return, and that is because of the cognitive bias known as reciprocation tendency, where you just want to return the favor. This is obviously something nice to do, but picture doing it on a business scale where you feel like you want to return the favor whenever a business deal provides you a profit; such a tendency can have catastrophic outcomes.

12. Stereotyping

You already know what stereotyping is, but you probably didn't know it was a cognitive bias. When you expect a person to behave in a certain way because of some preconceived notions about the group they belong to -for example, religion, color, sex, or creed- this is considered to be stereotyping. It is when you simply think that a person supposed to have similar or recurrent mannerisms because of some qualities they share with others without having any prior information on that person which warrants that conclusion. A few clear examples are assuming all women are grumpy or that all men are rough around the edges.

13. Social Comparison Bias

Remember that time a person around your age joined your company, but they were better looking, more competent, and just all-around more loved? Well, that might not even be the case, but this is what social comparison bias drives you to believe, and as a result, you end up unfairly biased against that person. Your brain makes you see that person as better than you, so you instinctively dislike them or assume they are annoying because of it.

14. Personal Validation Bias

This cognitive bias is quite common with religious individuals. It is when they assume something is true just because their beliefs demand it to be true, without actually considering the evidence or thinking it through. People with this cognitive bias will only consider information that carries a personal meaning or significance for them. They also tend to connect coincidences and perceive them as related because their beliefs and values demand it, even if there is no scientific or logical proof to back such claims.

15. Use It or Lose It Tendency

How many times have you learned a skill just for an interview or to impress someone? Or it could be because you had to learn it for school or a project. This tendency makes you learn such skills carelessly and rashly because you need to get it done, so it becomes much easier to lose it over time. When you take your time learning such skills, though, it becomes much easier to recall them when needed and much harder to forget what you have learned.

16. Survivorship Bias

This is when you focus on people or companies that survived a certain process and ignore those who didn't. This is why a lot of those self-development books you come across are basically nonsense. The whole "8 habits that will make you successful" deal doesn't make sense because yes, some successful people might have practiced those habits and succeeded. But what about those who didn't? Survivorship bias simply doesn't take into consideration any outliers, and it ignores the fact that correlation does not necessarily mean causation. In other words, just because two things are connected doesn't mean one is the outcome of the other. You won't necessarily achieve success by practicing certain habits, just because it worked for other people. There are several other factors at work here, like the person's own abilities and circumstances.

17. The Clustering Illusion

This cognitive error is when we tend to put too much stock into our perception of patterns that may be pure randomness. We see patterns where there simply aren't any, and this leads to errors in judgment and calculations that wouldn't happen if you didn't perceive randomness to mean something.

18. Courtesy Bias

Courtesy bias is one most of us do at one point or the other. It is when you give an opinion or a conclusion that does not necessarily align with yours, but you just do it out of courtesy in order not to offend people or hurt their feelings.

19. Continued Influence Effect

This cognitive bias is closely associated with confirmation bias. It is when you still think of wrong information or "facts" even after someone corrects you. A part of that misinformation lingers, and it could easily affect your judgment going forward. You try to come up with an explanation to confirm your beliefs, and when that fails, you still hold on to them and base your action on that.

20. IKEA Effect

Yes, there is actually a cognitive bias called the IKEA effect. It is when consumers trust or put too much stock into products they helped create, just like the Swedish furniture manufacturers' products that require some assembly on your end at home. The problem with this cognitive bias is the fact that it makes you overlook other angles to the product like quality and durability just because you will take part in creating it.

21. Information Bias

We talked earlier about the importance of information and how it can impact decision making and problem-solving, but we also mentioned that too much information could be quite problematic. Information bias is when your mind keeps looking for more details and asking questions when you don't need to. Seeking information where none is needed can be quite distracting and, thus, can impair your judgment. In other words, less information isn't always a bad thing, since quite often, the answer doesn't require all that data.

Logical Fallacies

1. Straw Man Fallacy

Starting with one of the most famous ones, straw man fallacy is one that happens quite often in arguments. It gives off the impression that a person is presenting a valid logical argument that refutes the other person's argument, while, in fact, they aren't.

What happens here is that the person basically refutes an argument that another didn't even present in the first place, giving the illusion of presenting a valid claim while it is, in fact, completely irrelevant. Therefore, it is said that the person engaging in this form of argument is attacking a "straw man". So, they basically knocked down this straw man rather than the opposing point of view.

For instance, person A says that marijuana should be completely legalized in all states because it does have medicinal uses and can help a lot of people. Person B replies by saying that person A wants to spread pot and illegal substances among young people and corrupt the citizens of the state. This is a straw man argument because this was not the initial notion presented, but it was taken out of context and blown out of proportion. Person B refuted a hypothesis that was not presented, rather than trying to refute the one presented.

2. Whataboutism

This is another very common logical fallacy, and it is when a person tries to discredit another person's claim by accusing them of hypocrisy for ignoring another subject rather than the one at hand, without trying to present a direct counterargument that is actually on point. If a person says that smoking is bad for you and people need to stop doing it, another may respond with "What about the pesticide-filled food you eat and the messed-up air you smoke because of pollution? Why don't you talk about those?"

As you can see, this rhetoric does not address the main argument presented but tries to discredit the person presenting it by calling them a hypocrite. In the example, the second person didn't say why smoking is good for you or why people should keep doing it, but they instead chose to accuse the other party of being hypocrites.

3. Ad Hominem

Ever been in an argument where someone personally attacked you instead of trying to present a valid argument of their own? Argumentum ad hominem is when another person questions the motives or character of the other side as a way to prove their point, which happens more often than we'd like to admit, especially in world politics. There are several types of this particular fallacy, but they are all centered on the same point, which is trying to undermine the person rather than their claims.

You make a claim that politician X is a good person because of reasons 1, 2, and 3, and in response another person says you are a xenophobe and racist because you support that politician. They could also say that politician is paying you to say those things, so they're questioning your motives and integrity here rather than refuting your claims with logical arguments.

4. Divine Fallacy

Remember that scene in Pulp Fiction where John Travolta and Samuel L. Jackson got shot at, and nothing hit them? Jackson's character said this had to be an act of God because it was so incredibly mind-blowing that this could happen. This is basically what a divine fallacy means; assuming something must be an act of God because there is no logical explanation. This also happens when unexpected diseases spread suddenly, so you find a lot of religious people claiming this as the divine wrath because of our sins, rather than trying to trace back the origins of the disease.

5. Argumentum ab Auctoritate

This is another heavily used and popular fallacy, translating to "appeal to authority" or "argument from authority". As you have probably figured it out from the translation, this is when a person uses the fact that their claim or argument is supported by a certain authority as grounds for its validity. This can be any sort of authority; religious, governmental, or even a manager at work. It happens quite often that you find a person making a claim that their viewpoint is valid because it was mentioned in their religious scripture or doctrine, or because some other form of authority figures states it.

6. Appeal to Consequences

This fallacy can be thought of as the outcome of wishful thinking. It is claiming that your beliefs are necessarily true because they bear good or acceptable consequences. It is basically appealing to a person's emotions rather than their logic and reasoning. A simple example would be saying that nothing bad ever happens to good people because they are good people, and it doesn't make sense for that to happen. You basically don't want it to be true because the consequences are not desirable or welcomed. This obviously does not make that statement true since the argument is based on emotions and wishful thinking rather than truths.

7. Appeal to Flattery

You probably have encountered this one quite often, and you might even do it on occasions yourself. Appeal to flattery is when you praise the listener or flatter them to make it easier for them to accept your argument. The centuries-old example would be the workplace, where workers use to appeal to flattery with their superiors to lure them into accepting new ideas or agreeing to something.

8. False Dilemma

This is when a person gives you an "either/or" situation when there is, in fact, other options that they are purposely or accidentally ignoring. They present you with two choices, claiming that one is false and, in turn, the other has to be true, when there might be more choices. Ever heard "If you're not with me, then you're against me"? This is an example of the false dilemma fallacy.

9. Guilt by Association

This fallacy is when you present an argument based on an invalid association or personal emotions which do not play into the final outcome of the question at hand. It is when, for instance, you believe we should all use plastic straws to protect the environment, and then you hear someone you dislike agreeing with you, so you dismiss your original point altogether. Or when a person who disagrees with your core beliefs presents a valid argument which you would normally agree with, but you reject it based on your feelings towards the person rather than the merits of what they propose.

10. Post Hoc

This is one of the most important ones mentioned in this list because the post hoc fallacy is one we often find ourselves dabbling in unknowingly. It is when you reason that just because one thing happened before another, then the first event is what caused the second. It is like saying that you got that job just because you took your wife's lucky bracelet that morning before heading to the interview. Or when you assume you have a fever because you went to the street the night before without a jacket on. While there is a correlation here, it doesn't necessarily imply causation.

Chapter Fifteen: How to Spot Bias in the Media

So, why exactly is it important to understand cognitive biases and logical fallacies? Because we're surrounded by them daily, and you are subjected to an unhealthy dose of fallacies and people's biases all day, and it is important that you understand how to deal with them and identify them.

We live in a highly polarized world, where people are extremely quick to pass snap judgments without considering the consequences of their actions. You turn on the TV or log onto social media only to be bombarded with crazy things happening around the world, and you feel the urge to give an opinion (or at least form one) just because your friends and peers are doing it. Therefore, critical thinking is crucial in this day and age. It is how you will be able to identify valid arguments you're presented with and weak ones you need to reconsider.

You must be able to spot bias in the media because we live in an age where media shapes our awareness and understanding of the world. Most people get their news and knowledge of the outside world through Facebook and Twitter, which is fine in itself. But you must be able to think critically of any piece of information you're exposed to so you can check its validity. How else can you form a valid opinion on an issue, without critical thinking and the ability to spot the bias? How would you vote? Who will you vote for? Which points of view should you adopt and advocate? These are all very important questions that you need to answer so you can form your opinions yourself, but first, you need to spot that bias in the media.

The Secrets to Spotting Bias in the Media

What Kind of News is It?

This is the first question you need to ask yourself if you want to spot bias in the media. Is it actual news, as in reporting something that has happened, locally or globally? Or is it an ad, or opinion piece? It is important that you assess the claim before doing anything because the form it takes will make a huge difference in how you should process and deal with it.

You will not read a piece of news from the same angle as you would an opinion piece. The first needs verification and double-checking; the latter will require those things, too, but it will also need you to look carefully at the person behind such opinion. Facts can be easily checked and vetted. Opinions, on the other hand, require more thought and consideration.

You should also identify whether or not the piece is offering an interpretation of facts, and this will need some careful consideration on your side because the interpretation of facts might offer some bias. This happens when the author uses a certain language to stir the viewer in a certain direction, or when they omit facts on purpose because it does not serve their point of view. Take this as an example: "The crime rate in South Africa has increased over the past few years, which shows that it is not a safe country." The first part of that statement is factually correct, but the second is not necessarily true. A person making a statement like that is using facts to support a possibly biased opinion. Therefore, it is important that you keep an eye out for such statements that might be misleading.

The Source

Now that you have identified what kind of information the news is, you need to have a closer look at the source. Question their motives. Is the source associated with some sort of political parties or persons of interest? This is particularly important in pieces related to certain individuals or groups. You must ask yourself whether or not the source behind the news has something to gain from this particular piece of information. The answer to that question will help you spot any potential bias.

There are news sources around the world known for being generally biased. They serve a particular agenda or aim to support a certain political or influential figure. You need to take any information from such sources with a grain of salt because they generally aim to misinform or guide the readers/viewers in a certain direction.

The Language

One of the easiest and most important ways through which you can spot bias in the media is through the language used. A person's language is quite an indication of what goes on in their minds –their beliefs and core values. Whenever you are absorbing any piece of news through the media, be wary of extreme language, because that often reveals a biased nature which is not reliable when it comes to news reporting.

You will find such people using extreme statements that are not subject to interpretation; it's often black-and-white with these guys, with no shades of grey possible. Words like best, worst, evil, and so on do not convey facts; they convey the person's own take and opinion on the matter, which goes against the purpose of unbiased news reporting. Using offensive language is obviously a clear indication that something is wrong here, and you have to consider what that source claims to be "facts" carefully. So, carefully examine the language and make sure it does not offer any biases.

The Evidence

What kind of evidence was presented to support the author's point of view? This is possibly the most important angle to spotting bias in the media. If a journalist writes an opinion piece, providing evidence, you will need to think about this evidence as much as possible so you could get to the bottom of this critically. For starters, does that evidence come from a reliable source, and has it been vetted? Or did the author just come up with a fictional source and cite them as the foundation for their argument?

You will also want to make sure that this evidence did a good job of covering the topic thoroughly and fairly, without leaving out any important context. Evidence can be misleading at times, and it can be missing or tampered with to misinform.

You also have to be able to see a clear connection between the evidence presented and the claims in the article or video. Does it make sense? Or is it farfetched? Sometimes, authors bring up completely irrelevant proofs to support their claim, and you would have to make huge leaps to connect the dots, which doesn't really say much about the validity of that evidence.

Is There Another Way to Look at This?

This question is as important as the evidence presented, if not more. Did the media piece leave room for other interpretations, or was it presented as absolute truth? As we have learned throughout the book, there are no absolute truths, and when a person claims their viewpoint is one, you need to stop and think about what they are saying. Scientific facts aside, anything can be refuted or presented with a counterargument, and it is your job to identify whether or not you are dealing with biased media.

Any story in the media can be interpreted from different angles if you are coming from a different background, and you need to put yourself in that place so you could question the authenticity and validity of the presented claims. If and when you get a feeling that the article or video is presenting just the single viewpoint, with no room for others, then there is something wrong there, and it might very well be biased. Ask yourself what is missing. Quite often, there is a certain piece of information or fact missing, and it is this one that could completely change your take on whether this piece is biased.

One thing you need to keep in mind, though, is that not all bias is bad. We are humans at the end of the day, and we have the biases that we cannot control. This is where critical thinking comes in. It will help you carefully analyze the piece of information you're dealing with and conclude as to whether the bias within this article or video affects the truths or tries to stir the reader in another direction. There is nothing wrong with taking sides at times; what counts is not trying to drive others to do the same - but letting them decide for themselves. Who knows, maybe after you're done considering the matter at hand from all angles, you will come to the same conclusion and share in that bias.

Chapter Sixteen: Managing Biased People and Winning Arguments

Understanding biases is only half the answer. How then are you going to deal with biased people? This isn't exactly an individual case you will come across every now and then. We encounter and deal with biased people every day of our lives because, again, it is just our nature to have certain preferences and biases. The catch is in identifying them, which you should be able to do by this stage in the book, and, more importantly, knowing how to deal with them.

Whether at work or in your personal life, you will stumble upon biased individuals, and you will often need to win the argument for whatever reasons. It is not exactly impossible to do so, but it will need some effort and consideration on your end, as well as critical thinking.

Identify the Bias

As we have repeatedly mentioned throughout this book, you cannot deal with a problem unless you have thoroughly identified and analyzed it. How do you expect to manage biased people if you don't even know what they're biased for? So, always make this your first step. Talk to the people you assume are biased, and before trying to win an argument with them, figure out what it is they have a problem with so you could base your argument on reasoning properly. It is very likely that you will find that this bias is because of a misunderstanding at the workplace, or even because you did indeed do something to elicit that particular bias out of people.

Focus on Your Own Attitude

For the most part, biased people might not present valid arguments. It will be full of logical fallacies and attempts to discredit your opinion or claim. It is crucial that you don't get dragged into such exchanges because this can be a slippery slope. You are someone who critically thinks about each and every argument they are presented with, and it is important to keep doing so even when you are faced with arrogance and disrespect.

More importantly, you need to think of the person in front of you as a rational being, meaning they can be persuaded if you present the proper argument. Don't take the easy way out and label them as idiots and walk away. Instead, try to try and show why you believe in what you have to say; show them evidence, and build a bulletproof argument so that they won't have any other option but to be persuaded.

Use Logic and Reasoning

Picking up from the last point, if you want to manage biased people and win arguments, you have to actually give an argument rather than try to attack the other person's argument. If you want to win an argument, leverage all the techniques you have learned throughout this book and try to build a solid foundation for your claim. You might be thinking right now, reading this, that you have done this before and still came out empty-handed. But the possibility of you failing to present a good argument is more likely than a good argument not yielding any good results. Quick comebacks and snarky remarks don't constitute an argument. You might think they make you look smart, and they even might, but they do nothing to further the debate or properly deliver your point of view.

It is also not about who presents their argument more emphatically, or loudly, but rather who backs their claims with logic. This is why we have been talking throughout the book about the importance of developing your reasoning and argumentative skills since they will help you in your life to become more persuasive by being able to deliver your viewpoints in a logical and reasonable manner. People will start listening to you a lot more because you will be convincing and a better communicator overall.

Using logic and reasoning to win an argument is a lot harder than it sounds because it requires you to back your claims with evidence and sound premises, and that takes effort. This is not something you can just do because you have one or two facts, and you'd like to build your whole argument based on those. For starters, understand that just because you have facts doesn't mean your argument is valid. The premises you are presenting have to add up to the conclusion, or else using them is pointless. For instance, if you say that fact one is "I am a human" and fact two is "Dogs are mammals", then the conclusion must be "I am a dog" is obviously faulty reasoning, despite using two correct premises. This is why it is important that you pay attention to the conclusion as much as to the truths presented, because they won't always add up, and you can't be making such arguments if you want to manage biased people.

Watch Your Language

When dealing with biased people, it is very important that you watch your language. Everything you say needs to be carefully weighed and considered because you might easily be feeding their biases and reinforcing what they already believe. No one wants to have to watch out for every word they say, but unfortunately, language does play a more important role in our lives than we think.

If you happen to be in a team meeting and all the language you have used consists of words like "oh, man, we have a lot of work to do" or "let's go, guys, we can do this", then you could easily be feeding the biases of some females on your team who believe you have a problem with women, because this is biased language you are using. You might not think much of it, but your words carry weight and meaning to others around you. The problem is, you might not even be remotely biased against women, but your subconscious is just used to using these words since they are the most used in society around you.

This is why it is important to have enough self-awareness to identify our own biased language. The first step to dealing with biased people and winning arguments with them is by looking at your own conscious or subconscious biases that might be feeding their beliefs. Once you do that and change your language, you will find that dealing with such individuals is much easier, and you are able to deliver your viewpoints while avoiding conflict.

Identify the End Goal

Why do you want to win this argument? What is the point of managing those particular biased people? These are the questions you must answer because they will dictate your behavior going forward. If it is a problem in the workplace, for instance, then you want to manage those people so you can avoid any conflicts around the office and have everyone do their jobs efficiently. So, it is not about your ego, and it is not about winning an argument for the sake of winning. You want those biased individuals to be satisfied, and it's not about just proving them wrong so you can sleep better at night. When you have the end goal in sight, you will be able to make much better decisions, and you will more easily win an argument –some by avoiding the argument in the first place because it reaps no rewards.

Offer Alternatives

A person who argues for the sake of arguing, without ever presenting alternatives, will never know peace of mind, and they will end up losing more arguments than they'd like. Again, it is not just about proving the other person wrong so you could win your argument and show that they are indeed biased. It is about presenting an alternative that would help them see where they went wrong and why this alternative is a better path for all to take.

At the end of the day, you want to help people achieve a certain goal, whether that is personal or professional, and if you just tear down their beliefs without offering alternatives, then what is the point? This is when people get defensive and shut out all you have to offer without any consideration since you were just busy with winning rather than showing them that there is a different way. If a person at work makes a claim or comes up with an idea that is faulty, don't just tear the idea down for the sake of doing it and to show that you are smart. Point out the flaws of that notion, and present alternatives that might better serve everyone's goals. Doing so, you will have won the argument and managed a biased person. And you might even win their approval and respect.

Chapter Seventeen: Identify and Outsmart Your Own Biases

The one question that remains is, how can you identify and deal with your own biases? Handling people with biases is easy, for the most part, and you can train yourself to spot and deal with them efficiently with sound reasoning. Your own personal ones are a whole different story, and yes, you do have plenty of personal biases of your own, because this is what it means to be human. We have preferences and likes/dislikes. This gets problematic if those preferences start affecting your judgment and impairing your decision-making skills. Throughout this chapter, you will learn the secrets and tips for identifying and outsmarting your own biases.

Pay Attention to Your Implicit Biases

You don't like right-wingers, for example. Your friends and family know it, and you are quite expressive and vocal about it. That is a bias of sorts, and it is not necessarily bad, because you are entitled to your beliefs. What is quite problematic, though, is the implicit biases that go through your mind without ever being expressed. Ever felt uncomfortable about seeing two people of the same gender kissing? Ever been around transgender people and felt uneasy? Ever been around a black person and felt a slight fear they might assault you? These are all internal biases that show an underlying problem. You might not be racist or homophobic per se, but you might display tendencies towards either or both, and the first step to dealing with that problem is acknowledging it exists.

You cannot outsmart your biases unless you are fully aware of their existence, and it is those implicit ones that you need to constantly be aware of so you can work on changing them. So, you could make a list of such situations like the ones we just mentioned and identify your implicit biases. Then, using critical thinking techniques you've learned throughout this book, deal with each problem separately until you can get to the bottom of this bias and whether or not it makes sense. This will help you get rid of your prejudices and start feeling at ease with people who have beliefs or orientations that are different than yours.

Accept Differences

Identifying that you have a problem with some "different" people is part of the answer. But you will also need to embrace those differences. Teach yourself to be tolerant of those who don't share your own beliefs and values. You could do it by talking to some of them or watching a program you hate because of some sort of bias. Overcoming your biases towards different people requires an effort because you need to seek them out and talk to them. Maybe you will start seeing that they aren't bad people, after all. In fact, they might be better than most in your life; they just don't share your belief system.

Be friendly towards them and try to feel less threatened. This will help you keep an open mind that embraces diversity and differences rather than shuns them. When you seek out those "different" people and try to really get to know them, you will learn that your biases don't make sense, and they have no solid foundation.

Beware of Positive Biases

Not all biases are negative; some can be positive. But that doesn't mean they are going to be positive for the other person. We tend to think of people in certain patterns and ways, and we often make them feel like they should adhere to our image of them. Not all Asian people are good with math and can help you with your technology problems, for instance. This might feel like a compliment to you and a rather positive stereotype, but who is to say your Asian friend would feel the same? Your black friend doesn't have to be athletic or good at basketball. Women don't need to be warm and caring, and they don't all have to be mothers.

These stereotypes and biases hurt people without you even knowing it. So, again, self-awareness is important here. Understand that people are under no obligation to live up to your image or stereotype of them and try to shatter these misconceptions and biases in the first place.

Consider the Possibility that You Might Be Wrong

It is a lot harder than it sounds. We tend to put too much stock in our intuition and gut feelings, which are often stemming from our very own biases. You need to start considering the possibility that you might be wrong, and you might be biased on occasions. When that happens, you will start reviewing your beliefs and core values, and critically think about your actions or decisions.

Overconfidence, as we mentioned earlier in the book, can be a very dangerous thing, and our faith in our own abilities can be intoxicating at times and could easily cloud our judgment. You are not infallible, and the sooner you realize that the better you will be able to identify and deal with your biases. Your intuition might be good, but it is flawed, and it rarely goes with evidence and facts. This is why you have to leave room for uncertainty. Yes, there might be occasions when you are under immense pressure to make a decision or come up with a solution, but you cannot rely on just gut feelings in times like that, because it will most definitely go with your biases. So, always assume that you might be wrong; it will open new doors for you and help you see things from a different perspective.

Listen to Those Around You

Want the best way to identify your biases and to outsmart them? Ask people! Believe it or not, your friends, family, and colleagues all have an opinion of you, and they probably think you have a bias or two. Now, what they say might be true, or it might not be. The important thing is that it will open your eyes to how people perceive you. Their take on your actions and decisions might lead you to identify some of your own biases that you were unaware of. Even if you don't immediately buy what they are saying, when you critically think it over and analyze your actions versus their claims, they might prove to be accurate. It might even confirm a suspicion you've had about your biases.

This is why it is important to include people in this process in one way or the other. Surround yourself with people that wouldn't be afraid to call you out on your errors in judgment and biases. To have biases is human, and sometimes you need help from other humans to identify those and deal with them.

Get Out of Your Comfort Zone

If you want to identify your biases, you need to get out of your comfort zone. Expose yourself to different people, as we have mentioned earlier, and expose yourself to media sources that can shine a light on some of your biases. How you react to certain news can give you a pretty accurate indication of what your personal biases might be. It might even help you overcome them as you see varying news sources covering one topic. When you critically think about such coverage, you will be able to go with what is right rather than what your personal biases are telling you is right.

One more thing you need to do to get out of your comfort zone is to make your biases known and explicit. Coming to terms with our shortcomings and flaws is never easy, but it is the only way you could ever deal with them. So, list your biases and take tests like the "*implicit association test*" to get an idea of just how biased you are, and towards what. It takes effort and discipline to learn whether or not you are prejudiced, but the outcome is certainly worth it.

Be Consistent

Use critical thinking to review your core beliefs and values constantly. Even if you think that you have reached the absolute truth and you have it all figured out, it is important that you go back to your roots regularly and deconstruct your views. You get a lot of input and information on a regular basis, and those will help you spot any biases you might have missed in the past.

Resources

https://www.verywellmind.com/lesson-three-brain-and-behavior-2795291

https://www.sciencedaily.com/releases/2018/11/181108142443.htm

https://opentextbc.ca/introductiontopsychology/chapter/3-2-our-brains-control-our-thoughts-feelings-and-behavior/

https://www.huffpost.com/entry/20-psychological-studies-_n_4098779https://www.youtube.com/watch?v=J0yEAE5owWw

https://www.criticalthinking.org/pages/a-brief-history-of-the-idea-of-critical-thinking/408

https://learn.filtered.com/blog/6-benefits-of-critical-thinking

http://www.umich.edu/~elements/probsolv/strategy/ctskills.htm

https://www.wabisabilearning.com/blog/useful-critical-thinking-mental-models

https://www.youtube.com/watch?v=krqMgqXRlas

https://www.youtube.com/watch?v=h-sm6qJUwfM

http://www.1000ventures.com/business_guide/crosscuttings/questions_socratic.html

http://www.ucdoer.ie/index.php/How_to_Ask_Questions_that_Prompt_Critical_Thinking

https://www.youtube.com/watch?v=IFWbxZrjWhM

https://www.wabisabilearning.com/blog/daily-critical-thinking-habits

http://futureofcio.blogspot.com/2014/11/the-noncritical-thinking-patterns.html

https://www.matiemedia.org/uncritical-thinking-is-dangerous-says-socratic-society/

https://www.edutopia.org/blog/critical-thinking-necessary-skill-g-randy-kasten

https://www.entrepreneur.com/article/228096

https://prezi.com/acmoxohoiyfl/problems-and-obstacles-in-problem-solving/

https://www.youtube.com/watch?v=QOjTJAFyNrU&t=65s

https://www.24alife.com/advice/stress/7-steps-in-resolving-problems

https://www.24alife.com/advice/stress/7-steps-in-resolving-problems

https://www.youtube.com/watch?v=QOjTJAFyNrU&t=65s

https://www.aesinternational.com/blog/5-common-mental-errors-that-affect-good-decision-making

https://medium.com/@georgejziogas/how-to-avoid-mental-errors-that-lead-to-poor-decisions-a20443de1a13

https://www.verywellmind.com/decision-making-strategies-2795483

https://hbr.org/2015/11/3-timeless-rules-for-making-tough-decisions

https://blog.kevineikenberry.com/leadership-supervisory-skills/four-steps-to-making-a-complex-decision/

https://www.verywellmind.com/steps-to-making-decisions-easily-20487

Dr. Paul Schempp:
https://www.youtube.com/watch?v=tCDkQNCVAlE

Dr. Joe Arvai: https://www.youtube.com/watch?v=NQ7SAcFp4so

Tony Robbins: https://www.youtube.com/watch?v=WVfrPTFJptM

Mikael Krogerus & Roman Tschappeler:
https://www.youtube.com/watch?v=KkyzYjPuxK8

Liv Boeree: https://www.youtube.com/watch?v=nisSeC81u2M

Dave Ramsey: https://www.youtube.com/watch?v=UUquj5onSVM

Nidhi Kalra: https://www.youtube.com/watch?v=nBCwlmMBmAQ

Peter Atwater: https://www.youtube.com/watch?v=TtJFBGooVeE

https://www.youtube.com/watch?v=lnMkHB0vNCE

https://www.psychologytoday.com/us/blog/finding-purpose/201810/what-actually-is-belief-and-why-is-it-so-hard-change

http://sourcesofinsight.com/where-do-beliefs-come-from/
https://en.wikipedia.org/wiki/List_of_fallacies
https://www.youtube.com/watch?v=Qf03U04rqGQ&t=261s
https://en.wikipedia.org/wiki/List_of_cognitive_biases
http://25cognitivebiases.com/
https://hatepseudoscience.com/2016/07/12/logical-fallacies-vs-cognitive-biases/
https://researchguides.njit.edu/evaluate/bias
https://blog.thinkcerca.com/how-to-spot-media-bias
https://hbr.org/2013/10/how-to-manage-biased-people
https://www.cornerstoneondemand.com/rework/5-tips-managing-unconscious-bias-work
https://www.youtube.com/watch?v=NKEhdsnKKHs
https://www.youtube.com/watch?v=VJZ8VHe2h0A
https://www.youtube.com/watch?v=TuUrB1025s0
https://www.sciencenewsforstudents.org/article/think-youre-not-biased-think-again
https://www.youtube.com/watch?v=GP-cqFLS8Q4
https://www.theguardian.com/women-in-leadership/2015/dec/14/recognise-overcome-unconscious-bias
https://www.psychologytoday.com/us/blog/in-practice/201508/6-ways-overcome-your-biases-good
https://www.fastcompany.com/90303107/how-to-become-a-less-biased-version-of-yourself
https://hbr.org/2015/05/outsmart-your-own-biases

Part 2: Cognitive Biases:

A Fascinating Look into Human Psychology and What You Can Do to Avoid Cognitive Dissonance, Improve Your Problem-Solving Skills, and Make Better Decisions

Introduction

The human brain is a complex device, and we still don't understand every one of its functions. In this book, we will take a look at a few functions that have to do with biases. You can find them in every corner of society, from the press to television, from the meeting room to the dining room. They have plagued us forever, but we are now starting to comprehend the threats they pose and understand them a little better.

On a more personal level, you can help fight these biases by being less biased. To do so, you need to identify your own biases, which is what I will show you how to do.

Let's be real here. We have all been there before. We had (or still have) poor thinking, decision making, and problem-solving abilities, and we have to clean up after the messes we've made.

But that ends today. Here, I will help you to identify and overcome your own biases and show you some thinking "hacks" to help you be a more effective thinker. It doesn't matter what your current strengths and weaknesses are in life. It does not matter if you let your emotions run free and control every aspect of your life. These things can be fixed, and you can do so without signing up for some complex training program, either.

Just take a moment now and imagine how simple life would be for you if you could just think and make decisions faster and without bias. We all want to be able to learn to do this. Now is the best time to get started.

SECTION 1: Psychology and the Human Mind

Brain Psychology: How Humans Think

Let's start from the beginning. To understand biases and other funny aspects of the human mind, you need to understand how our minds function. Don't worry. You won't get a dose of Psychology 101 here. We'll just cover basic information to give you a better understanding.

Have you ever wondered why we do things the way we do? Even though we strive to know ourselves, the reality is this—we don't know very much about our minds, and we know even less about how other people think. Charles Dickens once said, "A wonderful fact to reflect upon, that every human creature is constituted to be that profound secret and mystery to every other."

Psychologists have been working hard to study the human mind so they can find out how we see the world around us and understand what drives us into action. The brain is the most complex device, and the fact that something like this exists is a miracle. While the function of a single neuron in the brain can be understood and the general function of neural networks are vaguely grasped, the workings of the brain in its entirety is a mystery. So far, we have come a long way in understanding the brain, although there is still much to be learned. While different people have different mindsets and brain structures, we have learned, through many infamous studies and experiments, a few universal truths concerning human nature. Below are ten of those truths; truths that might just change your understanding of yourself.

Everyone Can Be a Little Bit Evil

Perhaps one of the most infamous experiments in the entire history of psychology is the Stanford prison study that took place in 1971. The study looked at the way human behavior is affected or influenced by social situations; a "prison" was created in the Stanford University psychology building basement by a group of researchers, led by Philip Zimbardo. Twenty-four undergrad students were then selected. None of them had any kind of criminal record, and all were healthy, in psychological terms. The students were to act as prisoners and prison guards, and they were observed by the researchers using hidden cameras.

While the experiment was meant to last for several weeks, it had to be stopped after less than one week. The prison guards were exhibiting extremely abusive behavior, not just physical but psychological torture, too, resulting in the prisoners becoming anxious and emotionally stressed.

Phillip Zimbardo went on record as saying, "The guards escalated their aggression against the prisoners, stripping them naked, putting bags over their heads, and then finally had them engage in increasingly humiliating sexual activities. After six days, I had to end it because it was out of control—I couldn't really go to sleep at night without worrying what the guards could do to the prisoners."

We Rarely See What's Right in Front of Us

Do you think that you know everything going on about you? You might do, but then again, it's more likely that you don't. None of us are every really fully aware. Back in the late 1990s, Kent and Harvard researchers tested people walking through the campus at Cornell University to see how well people noticed their immediate environment. During the test, an actor would go up to a person and ask for directions. As the person was providing those directions, the scientists would send two men with a wooden door who would walk in between the two, cutting them off from each other's view for some seconds. With no visual contact, the actor switched places with another actor, wearing different clothes, different hair, different voice, even with different height and build. About 50% of participants thought that the actor was the same person. They did not notice that they were talking to another actor.

So, what does this tell us? This was one of the original studies to explore the phenomenon called "change blindness." This goes to show that the human race is, on the whole, quite selective about the information they take in from our immediate environment or scene. It appears that we have a lot more reliance on pattern-recognition and memory far more than we realize.

It's Hard to Delay Gratification—But When We Do, We Experience Success

You might have heard of this experiment before. This was known as the famous Stanford marshmallow experiment that took place in the late 1960s. In this experiment, scientists wanted to see how preschool children resisted instant gratification when it was right in front of them. Instant gratification is the modern-day plague that kills off everyone slowly with an empty, unfulfilled life. From this experiment, scientists learned a lot about willpower and self-discipline. They put four-year-old children into an empty room and gave them a plate with a single marshmallow on it. The children were given a choice—eat the marshmallow now or wait for just 15 minutes. If they could wait, there would be two marshmallows.

Of course, we all know the best option would have been to wait and take the two marshmallows. The children knew that as well, and many of them chose to wait. The problem was that many of them could not resist, giving in and eating it before the 15 minutes' mark and forfeited the 2-marshmallow reward. Children who managed to control their urge and wait for the full length of time employed several tactics to avoid looking at the marshmallows—turning away from them, even covering up their eyes, so they didn't give in to temptation. There were a few significant implications of this behavior; those who can delay their gratification were not as likely to be overweight, or be addicted to alcohol or drugs, or even have any other behavioral issues when they grew up. What's more, is that they proved to be more successful in life.

It is Possible to Experience Conflicts in Our Moral Impulses

Do you know how far someone might go to comply with authority and rules when they are asked to hurt others? In 1961, a study conducted by Yale psychologist Stanley Milgram answered this question. You may not like the answer because the internal conflict of harming others against your own personal morals and any obligation you feel in bowing down to authority causes what is known as cognitive dissonance. I will cover it in a later part of this book.

In this study, Milgram was looking to gain information about why Nazi war criminals did what they did during the holocaust. After all, how could someone do something so evil? Were they inherently evil individuals, or were they just victims of their own circumstances?

So, Milgram tested two participants at a time, one being labeled as the "teacher" and the other labeled as the "learner." Next, the teacher was asked to give the learner some questions, and if the learner answered incorrectly, then he or she would get increasingly powerful electrical shocks; the more questions they answered incorrectly, the worse the shocks got. The teacher was in a different room from the learner, so they could not see what was really going on. The learner was not actually subject to electrical shock, though; instead, Milgram just played recordings to simulate painful screaming. The test was to see what the teacher would do when forced to do something against his will. The teachers would request to stop the experiment, but the researchers would encourage them to continue.

The result came, and it showed that up to 65% of the teachers went up to a maximum of 450V shock. Many of them were visibly distressed and uncomfortable.

What does this experiment tell us? For one, it shows the dangers of blind obedience to authoritative figures. However, some argued the results highlight a deep moral conflict, not blind obedience.

Since humans are social animals, we learn to adapt to other humans around us so we can fit in. That means we have a natural tendency to be good to other people in our group. We also developed a tendency to be hostile to those outside our group. So, the moral conflict here occurs because of association. The teacher can empathize with the student being "shocked," but he was on the researcher's side, so he felt the need to continue to administer electrocution even though he did not feel comfortable doing it.

In the end, it does not matter how one interprets the result. The fact is, some would go all the way to administering a 450-volt shock to another human being just because another person with authority told them to.

Power Can Easily Corrupt Us

Three things can create a tyrant: wealth, power, and fame. Some people can suddenly turn bad when they experience one of those. Sometimes, even your colleagues suddenly start to act all high and mighty after a promotion to a higher position. There is a psychological reason behind this sudden shift in behavior.

In 2003, a study was published in a journal called *Psychological Review*. In this study, the participants were students, and they were divided into groups of three. Each group was tasked to write a short paper together. Since this was a group effort, a group leader was needed, and so one of the three took that position. Two out of each group had to write that paper while the third was asked to judge it and work out how much compensation the writers should get. The researchers did not study so much the effect of the amount of money that would be compensated. This was only done to give the third student, the designated boss of the group, the power that befits the position.

While the groups were working, a researcher would occasionally bring a plate containing five cookies into the room. Further observation showed that the final cookie was almost never eaten, which is still a common sight nowadays. Other than that, they also found that the boss in the group was nearly always the person to eat the fourth cookie, and they often did so in a sloppy manner.

Other than that, the boss of each group was also more likely to touch others, sometimes inappropriately, flirt more directly, make riskier choices, and was often the first person to make an offer in negotiations, the first to voice their opinions, et cetera. Basically, when the students were given more power in the group, they became more open, direct, and daring.

We Seek Loyalty from Our Social Groups and Are Drawn to Conflict Easily

We have had two World Wars and countless armed conflicts between states and between smaller social groups throughout human history. Even with so many deaths, you would think that we would have had enough of war for the entirety of human history, right? Not really. The only reason why World War III hasn't started yet is because of Mutual Assured Destruction (MAD), which is a deterrence against nuclear states from just nuking each other. But I'm not going to discuss MAD here. What I want to explore is the reason why we get involved in conflicts so frequently, and then we become friends with each other so soon, as if nothing happened. A social psychology experiment from the 1950s could provide us with an answer to that.

In this study, volunteer boys aged 11 were divided into two groups. One was called the Eagles, and the other was called the Rattlers. They were taken to Robbers Cave State Park in Oklahoma, and the boys were told that they were going to be at summer camp. The two groups were not aware that the other existed, and they each spent the week in a different part of the camp, engaging in fun activities and forming bonds within their respective groups.

Then, the second phase kicked in, and the groups were brought together. The two groups had certain differences, and it did not take long before conflicts started to happen. First, the name-calling started, and then, researchers introduced competitive games that pitted the two groups against each other, which led to more conflicts.

In fact, it got so bad that the two groups got to the point where they would not eat together. But that was not the end of it.

The scientists then decided to try and bring the two groups together. First, they introduced fun activities that both groups could enjoy together, which did not work well. Then, they went ahead and had the boys solve problems together, which worked, and the two groups were a little closer at the end.

What do we learn here? Different social groups are more likely to cooperate with one another when they share a common *problem*.

We Need Just One Thing for Happiness

We hear this all the time. In fact, we might have said it to ourselves at some point in our lives. "Oh, if only I had 'X,' then I would be happy forever." In reality, we always want more and more. I'm talking about material possessions, fame, and power. They could never make us happy. There is only one thing that can grant us happiness, and it was the Grant Study at Harvard University that showed us what it was—a study that lasted 75 years!

In this study, researchers enlisted 268 male subjects from Harvard who were undergraduates. The subjects would be followed and observed for the next 75 years, with data from different bits of their lives being collected at regular intervals.

At the end of the study, researchers determined that at the end of the day, the only thing that really matters is love. That's not to say that power, money, and fame are worth nothing; they are worth something, but you don't need them to live—the only key to long-term happiness is love.

George Vaillant was the director of the study, and he said that love has two primary pillars—happiness only comes when you can find love and when you live your life in such a way that you allow love in. This goes a long way toward explaining why some antisocial people or those who choose to live an isolated life are typically unhappy. They do not let themselves interact with others, and that means love cannot find its way into their lives.

What was amazing about this study was one of the 268 subjects. He was considered by the scientists to be the worst out of all of the subjects. He had the lowest future stability rating. In fact, he was so low that he even attempted to commit suicide. But he eventually came through and became one of the happiest people out of all the subjects. How did he make such a recovery? It was love. He spent his life looking for love.

Social Status and Strong Self-Esteem Help Us to Thrive

There's no doubt that success and fame can give our egos a big boost; it's obvious, but there is more to it than that. There is a school of thought that says self-esteem provides longevity; at least, that's what was claimed by the Oscar Winners study.

Researchers studied directors and actors who were recipients of Academy Awards and, in the process, discovered that they lived, on average, four years longer than those who got a nomination but didn't win.

That doesn't tell us an awful lot really; after all, the winners may just have had a healthier lifestyle, or it could just have been nothing more than dumb luck. However, it does provide some correlation with this theory, although we really don't know if being lucky enough to win an Academy Award can add another four years to your life—don't quit your day job just yet!

What we did learn was that social factors have a role to play in longevity. Self-esteem definitely helps to improve health, and although it may sound like nothing more than pseudoscience, it does kind of make sense. What it really boils down to is this—the more happiness we feel, the longer our lives are, and, as we already know, the key to happiness is love.

We Try to Justify Every Experience so It Makes Sense

This comes under something we'll discuss more in part 2—cognitive dissonance—but it is something that any student of Psych 101 class should be familiar with. All humans will naturally try to avoid any psychological conflict between their actions and their thoughts or beliefs, and, for this, we'll look at a study that psychologists Leon Festinger and Merrill Carlsmith carried out in 1959.

Study subjects were asked to do a series of tasks. These were boring tasks, and they were asked to do them for an hour or so. Each subject would then be given $1 or $20 to say that the tasks were interesting when they clearly weren't. Festinger discovered that the subjects paid $1 enjoyed these boring tasks more than those paid the higher amount. You would think it would be the other way around, so why wasn't it?

It turned out that the subjects who were paid $20 felt that the money was justification enough for doing those tasks and, as such, could be more objective. The subjects who were only paid $1 didn't have sufficient justification for being objective. Cognitive dissonance needed reducing, so the subjects had to find some way of justifying how they behaved; they did this by claiming that the tasks were fun to do.

It boils down to this—we tell ourselves lies so that things appear more logical than they actually are.

We Find it Easy to Buy into a Stereotype

We all stereotype to a certain extent, as hard as we try not to, and it can result in coming to unfair conclusions about people, ethnic groups, classes, entire populations even, and that is potentially very harmful. As an example, we'll look at a study carried out by John Bargh, an NYU psychologist.

He conducted experiments on social behavior and how automatic it is, concluding that, very often, we judge other people based entirely on stereotyping, even though we usually do it unconsciously. More often than not, we do nothing to stop ourselves from doing it.

Humans also tend to buy into social stereotypes, particularly for groups that they are not involved in or a part of. Bargh gave a group of study participants some words that were to do with old age, like "wrinkled" and "helpless," asking them to unscramble those words. Another group was given another set of words, not related to age. Of the two groups, the one that worked on the age-related words walked much slower after the test than the other group. He took the experiment a step further, still using two groups of people, with words related to politeness and race—his findings concluded that we unconsciously enforce stereotyping.

According to Bargh, stereotypes are simply categories that have been pushed too far. He also said that, with stereotypes, we tend to take in the qualities of that stereotype, like age, gender, color of the skin, etc., and our minds will automatically respond with labels, such as hostile, weak, strong, friendly, etc. Those labels do not, in any way, reflect on reality and are purely an unconscious response, based on what we think we know.

Brain vs. Mind: Know the Difference

If you don't have a degree in neurobiology, you're forgiven for thinking that the brain and the mind are the same thing. We use the two terms interchangeably, and in most contexts, this is fine. But when one intends to study the complex system of the human mind, one needs to be able to make a distinction between the brain and the mind.

Here's an example. When you stub your toe, what do you say? Most likely, "I stubbed my toe, and it hurts like hell," and not "The pain receptors in my toe light up and send a signal that travels through my leg, up my spine, to my brain to let it know that the toe just had a collision with a foreign object."

The first response is the mind speaking, whereas the brain does the talking for the second response.

Simply put, the mind is synonymous with our thoughts, feelings, memories, and beliefs. The mind is the source of our behaviors. It is formless, but it is very powerful. On the other hand, the brain is physical and is the source of the mind.

When you experience an emotion or have a thought, the brain lights up certain neurons, and the mind interprets those signals to formulate those thoughts or emotions.

But the distinction is still a debate today. While neuroscientists do not object to discussing the mind in casual conversations, many insist that the mind is not real or distinct from the brain. The idea that the mind is an independent entity from the brain is unacceptable. On the other hand, civilians embrace the distinction, as mind training, such as mindfulness and meditation, has been proven to have positive effects on the brain.

Nonetheless, the debate still rages on today, and the outcome will have far-reaching consequences.

For now, you can believe that the "mind" doesn't exist and whatever you think and feel is just a bunch of neurons in your brain lighting up. Alternatively, you can think of the brain as the computer—the hardware—whereas the mind is the software—the software/system—both of which work in conjunction.

Heuristics: How We Make Decisions

Heuristics is nothing more than a mental shortcut, saving us potentially hours of time in making simple decisions. Heuristics allow us to make quick decisions, which is practical, although it does not guarantee to be the optimal, perfect, or even rational decision. It can at least allow us to reach a short-term goal.

Heuristics are often used when finding the best solution to a problem is impractical or outright impossible. They help speed up the process and take away some of the load from making a decision. Heuristics are commonly used in the following situations:

• **Consistency Heuristic** - when situations are responded to in consistent ways.

• **An Educated Guess** - when a conclusion is reached, even without enough information or research. A person considers what they learned in the past and relates it to a current situation, applying what they think they know, even though it may not be correct.

• **Absurdity Heuristic** - an absurd approach to any situation, when a claim is made that is unlikely, and not based on common sense.

• **Common Sense** - applied to problems or situations based on observation; a practical approach allowing a quick decision to be made when the wrong and right answers are clear.

• **Contagion Heuristic** - when a person avoids something he or she believes is not good. An example would be if a product he or she bought is recalled because of a defect; they may then opt to never purchase from that company again, to avoid the same problem arising in the future.

- **Availability Heuristic** - when a situation is judged based on previous situations similar to it, and a person can apply their previous experience to the current situation.

- **Working Backward** - a method of finding a solution to a problem by understanding what the desired solution is and working back to determine how to arrive at the solution. An example would be a maze game—you know you have to get to the center, you just have to work out how to do it, and the easiest way is to work backward from the center.

- **Familiarity Heuristic** - when someone approaches a problem in the same way that they have approached similar problems in the past, to reach a predictable and similar result.

- **Scarcity Heuristic** - when we want something because it is scarce, suggesting that we place a higher value on scarcity or rarity.

- **Rule of Thumb** - a simple, yet broad approach to solving problems, whereby we make an approximate decision or draw an approximate conclusion, with little need for research.

- **Affect Heuristic** - when a quick impression is used to base a solution or decision on. This is often a helpful heuristic, particularly when in a life or death situation; we can make an immediate decision without the need for research, but, if applied to the wrong situation, this heuristic can cause harm.

- **Authority Heuristic** - when a person believes that another person's opinion is true purely because they are a figure in authority. We tend to see this applied more in politics, science, and education.

It is worth pointing out that overreliance on heuristics can lead to fallacy and biases, which I will cover in the next part.

SECTION 2: Cognitive Biases

What Are Cognitive Biases?

We are going to explore various biases, both conscious and unconscious, in many contexts such as the workplace, the family, and society at large. This is where things get interesting. Understanding and acknowledging that you have biases is the first step to becoming less biased.

Think of cognitive biases as faults in our thinking systems. We tend to think in a logical, objective way. Cognitive biases are the patterns that stray from that norm or rationality. Most of these biases can be reproduced, and therefore confirmed, by research, but there are often controversies about how one should go about classifying or explaining them.

While biases come in many forms, we can categorize them into two main groups known as "cold" or "cognitive" biases and "hot" or "motivational" biases. The former is all about information, such as neglect of probability, distinction bias, or anchoring. It is simply a miscalculation. The latter is more emotionally-driven, such as wishful thinking. What is more important to note is that both hot and cold biases may be present at the same time.

There are many controversies over the interpretation of biases. I will show you later because some believe that they are not irrational; or that they may lead to useful attitudes or behavior. For instance, let's look at leading questions. When getting to know others, people often ask leading questions, which appear to be biased toward confirming their assumptions about the person. Many argue that this kind of confirmation is simply a way to establish a connection with the other person, so it is simply a social skill, which is not bad in any way.

Of course, when one discusses cognitive biases, one cannot overlook the importance of heuristics. Simply put, a heuristic is a mental shortcut that allows us to make quick and efficient decisions. Heuristics help us shorten decision-making time and allow us to go from day to day without having to stop to think about what to do next.

Quick and efficient heuristics can also lead to cognitive biases. After all, just because something works once does not mean that it will work every time. The best example here are jokes or lies. You tell it once, and it might work, but it won't work the second time around. So, if you rely on heuristics too much, you may not see other alternatives that may be better options. Heuristics can also introduce stereotypes and prejudice because we use mental shortcuts to classify and categorize people, thus overlooking the smaller details. We tend to end up generalizing.

What Are Logical Fallacies?

A logical fallacy is a flaw in one's logical arguments that undermines their validity. Certain logical fallacies appear sound, but they are still fallacies, and it is best to keep an eye out for these subtle variants.

Again, because of the variety of structures and applications, fallacies are difficult to classify in a way that satisfies all practitioners. One can classify them based on their structure or content, divided into subcategories, the processes, et cetera. Below are some of the most common fallacies:

1. Straw Man Fallacy: This is one of the most common tactics people employ to win debates. Basically, they will over-simplify or purposely misrepresent or frame your arguments in a way that makes it easier for them to attack. But that does not mean that they fully address your actual argument. They simply create an easier target, a "straw man," which hopefully convinces other people that this accurately represents your argument. The best way to know whether a person is using this approach is when they begin by saying, "So you're saying." The best strategy is to not respond to the attack on the straw man and reiterate what you were saying.

2. Bandwagon Fallacy: Basing the validity and soundness of one's argument on popularity, or a representation of this popularity (four out of five people recommend "X", et cetera.) This is because the argument does not take into consideration whether the population validating it is qualified to do so.

3. Appeal to Authority Fallacy: While appealing to authority is a sound argument in many cases, relying on it too much can be dangerous, especially if the source of authority is trying to validate something outside its expertise. The simplest case here would be to say that the head of the IT department cannot validate an argument related to the finance department.

4. False Dilemma Fallacy: When someone misleadingly presents a complex issue and offers two mutually exclusive options. It's either "A" or "B" and no in-between. The two options are often on extreme ends of the spectrum, thus ignoring all the possibilities in-between that allow for compromises.

5. Hasty Generalization Fallacy: A general conclusion is drawn from a very small sample size. Just because two people in the entire company report higher productivity from meditation does not mean that the company should impose mandatory meditation sessions.

6. Slothful Induction Fallacy: This is the opposite of the previous fallacy. Basically, even with enough evidence that represents the entire population, one does not acknowledge the validity and soundness of the argument.

7. Correlation/Causation Fallacy: Correlation or causation is when two or more things happen in a given situation, and one event has an impact on the other. For instance, hot sunny days cause sunburn and increase the consumption of ice-cream. The cause is the sunny day, and the ice-cream and sunburn both occur because of this. However, one has the correlation/causation fallacy when they incorrectly claim that ice-cream causes sunburn.

8. Anecdotal Evidence Fallacy: Arguing from one's own experience rather than logical evidence, thus taking one possible isolated example as proof and ignoring the overwhelming proof to the contrary. This fallacy is often seen in cases against vaccination.

9. Texas Sharpshooter Fallacy: This comes from a Texan who shot at the wall of his barn and then painted a large target around the nearest grouping of bullet holes. Then he said that this was proof of his marksmanship. Basically, the person cherry-picks data to support their own argument and ignores a plethora of proof that supports the contrary.

10. The Burden of Proof Fallacy: The burden of proof will always rest on those who make a claim. If someone claims that something is true, then they need to prove it. If there's no evidence presented against it, that doesn't mean it's true.

20 Cognitive Biases

In addition to the logical fallacies we've discussed above, here are 20 common cognitive biases that can interfere with your decision-making:

1. Availability Heuristics: Basically, we see the big terrifying events to be more serious than the more common ones. For instance, many people view plane crashes to be something very scary indeed, but they do not take into consideration that more people die in car accidents than plane crashes. It's true that a plane crash can take 300 souls with it, but deadly or serious car crashes occur a lot more often.

2. Halo Effects: Because our brains love consistency, we believe that when we see one quality in a person, we think that the rest should be just as consistent. Looking for contradictions within a person can be tiring, so we use this heuristic, which turns out to be a bias. The best example is this: "The first impression lasts a lifetime." Basically, when you walk into an interview and make a positive first impression straight away, the interviewer will take you more seriously and view you in a good light, thus increasing your chance of landing that job, even if you have some flaws in other areas. Your positive first impression casts a hazy halo of positivity over all other information.

3. Sunk Cost: To sum this up, it's over-commitment. This is the belief that once we have sunk enough time and resources into something, we are less likely to abandon it, even if the project at hand will fail. Instead of cutting our losses and pulling out early, this bias leads us to keep trying even though it's already doomed, resulting in the loss of more time and resources.

4. Survivorship Bias: We all love success stories. We've known many figures that decided to drop out of college and decided to start up their own tech company, which ended up being multi-billionaire corporations. Many of us know that this is a very risky move, yet these success stories tell us that it is possible, and the ROI is enormous, so we are blinded to the actual probabilities. In this case, we see Mark Zuckerberg, Bill Gates, and Steve Jobs being successful as dropouts, but we do not consider countless other dropouts who are struggling from day to day. Of course, you can possibly strike it rich as an entrepreneur, but the chances are very, very slim.

5. Action Bias: The tendency to choose action over inaction in the face of ambiguity even though taking action is counterproductive. This bias can present itself when people have to make decisions while under pressure, such as in a competitive environment.

6. Framing Bias: This occurs when someone is influenced by how the information is presented, but not the information itself. For example, one could represent an economic downturn between the years 2009 and 2011, even though the economy began to improve again then after the global financial crisis.

7. Strategic Misrepresentation: This bias occurs when someone is being too optimistic and underestimates the cost or risk of their decisions. This often occurs when someone is passionate about their innovative ideas and wants to put them forward and get them into action as soon as possible without conducting enough research to test their viability. It's either that or the person fully understands the risks associated with their ideas, but they have decided to go ahead with them anyway because they "know it will work."

8. Ambiguity Bias: This is similar to action bias. Basically, when a person is faced with a lack of information, their default option would be to stick with what they already know. This is usually a good move, especially when the risks outweigh the benefits, but this can also inhibit innovations as it is in their nature to be unknown and risky.

9. Pro-Innovation Bias: This occurs when there is a belief that something new and innovative needs to be adopted by literally everyone in the team, company, social group, or entire populations. The problem here is that since everyone is inherently different, forcing a new and largely untested concept upon them is never a good idea. But this bias makes innovation look like something that is desirable and inherently good so that all the potential negative impacts fade into obscurity. Those with this bias may not see problems such as sexism, elitism, and inequality that could result from their innovative ideas.

10. Status-Quo Bias: Also known as the "fear of change," people with this bias tend to favor the current situation and do nothing about their circumstances; simply, they are afraid that they may lose something, even though sometimes the only thing they'll lose is their chains. This bias can trap people in a detrimental situation and keep them there for the rest of their lives unless they see the errors in their ways and work to get out of there. This bias is especially subtle because it aligns with the fact that our brains love consistency. The best way to spot this bias is when someone refuses to do something simply because "It's not the way we do things around here," rather than offering a valid reason.

11. Feature Positive Bias: This bias is very similar to strategic misrepresentation bias. People with this bias tend to look at what they stand to gain from an option rather than considering what they could lose from it. This can occur due to limited time and resources that prevent them from thinking objectively, so they then develop a tendency to hope for the best.

12. Affinity Bias: The tendency to favor people who are like ourselves. Birds of a feather flock together, after all.

13. Belief Bias: The tendency to believe that one's argument is logical and sound—not because of the supporting evidence, but by relying on one's own beliefs over the truth of the conclusion.

14. Empathy Gap: The tendency to underestimate how emotions play a role in all aspects of life, in either oneself or others.

15. Hard-Easy Effect: The tendency to view one's own ability as adequate when one has to accomplish hard tasks and inadequate when one has to accomplish easy tasks.

16. The Illusion of Control: The tendency to overestimate one's own control over external events.

17. Hot-Hand Fallacy: The tendency to overestimate the chance of success is higher simply because that person or group has been successful (by luck rather than judgment) in the past. If you have studied probability, the chance of flipping a coin and getting heads five times in a row is substantially lower than getting it three times in a row.

18. Self-Serving Bias: This is similar to confirmation bias, which I will get to, because it is the tendency to evaluate ambiguous information in a way that benefits a person's interests. It is also a tendency to claim more responsibility for success than failures.

19. Hindsight Bias: Also known as the "I-knew-it-all-along" effect, is the tendency to see past events as being predictable. While this bias does not display itself during the decision-making process and therefore is harmless at that stage, it does prevent people from acknowledging their mistake, learning from it, and therefore preventing similar problems from happening in the future.

20. Confirmation Bias: Characterized as the tendency to look for or interpret information in such a way that supports one's own arguments or views, while also discrediting other evidence that supports the contrary. This bias is related to cognitive dissonance, which we will discuss in the next chapter.

Unconscious Biases: They're All Around You

To prove that unconscious biases exist, let's do a quick test. Go onto Google and type: CEO. Look at the top results. More often than not, you will see that there are more images of men in suits than women. Now, you may not see what is going on there, and you're forgiven for that. This is why these things are called "unconscious biases." Many people do not notice these small things in life, although they are just as dangerous to our cognition. The fact that I pointed this out may make me look like I'm nitpicking, but hear me out. What you are looking at is sexism in its most subtle form. Small things like images can reinforce certain stereotypes and demonstrate sexism inherent in our society. These small things are known as "unconscious" or "implicit" biases. Many people would not even notice these subtle things unless we were the ones being discriminated against, or if the images otherwise failed to represent us. These hidden biases and stereotypes impact small things such as designs, images. Though small as they are, they still reinforce biases and are, therefore, just as dangerous.

Unconscious bias (also known as implicit bias) only got its name back in 2006. It started out as a study on the unconscious mind. More specifically, the unconscious mental processes that lead to various problems such as discrimination in governmental institutions and the justice system. This field of study does not accept what was once a long-held belief that our behaviors are only influenced by external or explicit factors such as conscious thoughts or beliefs.

You can find examples of unconscious biases everywhere. The neighborhood that you live in, the people you hang out with, and those who you love. It is inevitable, and everyone has it to varying degrees. Developments in neuroscience now show that biases are formed as we grow up, meaning that we start to develop biases from childhood. To make matters worse, these biases are formed and ingrained at the subconscious level, and they are often reinforced through societal and parental conditioning.

Since we gather countless information and our brain needs to process all of that data, it unconsciously develops ways to categorize and format the data into familiar patterns, so it can process all the data effectively. Those familiar patterns are, of course, unconscious biases. No matter how hard we try to avoid it, we do it all the time. Things like gender, ethnicity, disability, sexuality, body size, professions, etc. all influence our initial impression of another person, and this forms the basis of our relationship with them.

As mentioned before, unconscious bias can be found in many places. Below are three main places to be aware of your biases and how you can deal with them.

In the Workplace

Biases in the workplace are pretty common, especially if the company is not so inclusive. Here are some things you can do to combat biases in the workplace:

Pause Before You Speak

The expression "Turn your tongue seven times before speaking," applies here. This isn't because you need to loosen up the tongue so you can speak properly, but rather to give yourself time to think about what you are actually going to say. This is a cure for what is called "foot-in-mouth syndrome."

A lot of people make the mistake of speaking their mind without practicing the care to select their words carefully. This is when the unconscious biases surface because the brain uses the same bias-ridden system to articulate our thoughts. Unless you consciously select your words, then whatever is coming out of your mouth may sound prejudiced or discriminatory.

There was a journalist whose name I shall not mention, although you may know her already. She thought of what seemed to her to be a funny joke and then tweeted it, saying something along the lines of "I'm going to Africa. I'm afraid of getting AIDS. Oh, wait, I'm white." To her, it was an innocent joke, but it ended up ruining her entire career, and everyone ripped her apart on the Internet.

So, before you speak, let alone make a joke, stop and think how others will interpret your own words. More often than not, people will interpret them in the most negative way possible (partly thanks to their own biases).

The rule of thumb here is: "When in doubt, just don't."

Validate Others' Experiences

Everyone has a different past, so they will have their own sets of beliefs, values, behaviors, and experiences. Accept the fact that it is okay to be different. It really doesn't matter if everyone works together to achieve a common goal anyway. Respect differences. In fact, having a diverse group of people on the team may be helpful, because some of them may have unique ideas that may solve the problem at hand.

Stop to Listen

Ask yourself: how often do you ask a question to which you think you already know the answer? The answer is mostly like to be quite often, and if so, you're either a lawyer, very smart, or you have unconscious bias. Again, this is something that people do all the time. Here's another question: how often do you ask for suggestions from other people although you've already made up your mind?

This is quite common in the workplace. In the corporate world, efficiency is highly valued as it keeps production up and costs down. Unfortunately, speedy decisions are often not recommended.

So, the next time that you ask a question, just listen to what others have to say. Ask follow-up questions if you need to. You might learn a thing or two from other people.

Connect with People Who Are Different to You

Make a habit of seeking out ideas from other people before you voice yours, especially if they have a different perspective from yours. You might want to extend the circle of friends you hang out with if possible because if you have been hanging with the same people for a long time, then you won't learn much more from them.

You want to have a circle of friends from various backgrounds. Whenever there is a discussion, allow and encourage other people to voice their opinions first because they may have something good to say. Keep an eye out for the people who usually do not talk much during meetings. I recommend you seek out their advice and opinions. You might be surprised to hear what they have to say.

Demonstrate Your Support

You should back up your beliefs with actions. If you are an advocate for equality and diversity, then you want to support those who are being discriminated against. If you see someone being bullied in the workplace, stand up for them, and do not be afraid to call the other person out for their unacceptable behavior. Make sure you are polite when you tell them about it, though. More often than not, that person may not know that they are discriminatory. Give them the benefit of the doubt. Just make sure to let them know that their behavior is unacceptable.

At Home/in the Family

We live in a society that constantly changes, so children need to learn how to cope. The biggest thing right now is diversity, and children need to learn how to live with people who are inherently different from them.

Since external factors easily influence children, the responsibility lies with you and others around them to teach them everything they need, and that also includes how not to be biased. The only issue here is that children will interact with other people who are also biased, and they can pass their false beliefs to children.

So, in light of all this, what can we do to help children overcome biases? The best way we know so far is by talking to them about the issue and helping them to understand the situation by having them empathize with the victim. Avoiding "the talk" is going to cause many problems down the road because, again, children look for nonverbal cues that we often unconsciously display. By making it clear with them, they will be a lot less likely to develop biases.

In Society

In society at large, biases are everywhere, especially sexism—both implicit and explicit. Take politics, for example. Back in 2008, both Sarah Palin and Hilary Clinton fell victim to misogyny when they ran for Vice President and President, respectively. Both of them were subject to various vicious comments, and most of these run-ins did not have anything to do with their campaigns. This begs the question, would they have been treated differently, had they been men?

Gender bias is also prevalent in the media. Many women say that they are not accurately reflected in the media; such as television, film, advertisements, broadcast news, et cetera. Although the situation is improving, it is not nearly as fast as it should be, and that is probably only because a small percentage of the media decision-makers, those with enough power to approve which content to put up, are female. Right now, some traditional media outlets are improving how they handle bias, although some say that it is not enough, and there are a number of specialized outlets that do a better job.

But it's not just the news media, either. There are also issues with other types of programming, such as mainstream cinema, which has a lack of diversity in its characters and stories and has a notoriously low number of women with spoken lines in most cases.

Thankfully, women's issues are at the forefront of our cultural dialogue, at least in the United States. We have made great progress over the last few decades as advocates continued their efforts in pushing against these longstanding biases. If people stop speaking out, then these problems will persist.

Beating Your Own Biases

If you want to be less biased and a little less prejudiced, then there is good news and bad news. The bad news is that we are naturally biased, because the only way we can make sense of the world is through generalization and putting things and people into mental categories that our minds create on their own. These categories can imply good and bad things. A human with zero bias is a human that just cannot function because they waste a lot of time trying to experience the world from an objective standpoint, making no inferences or assumptions. What does this look like in practice? Not taking a flight because you do not trust the pilot or not assuming that the other person who has their knife at your throat has malicious intent.

So far, scientists have found no way to eradicate prejudice completely, so all of the grant money that went into the research may have been for naught. There is just no proven way to make people completely unbiased, unless we replace the brain with a supercomputer. This brings about many more problems related to cybernetically-enhanced humans or artificial intelligence, but we're not going to discuss that here.

On the flip side, the good news is that while it is impossible to eliminate bias and prejudice, these two are not absolute states, meaning that one can have varying degrees of both, partly thanks to parental and peer conditioning and previous experience. The fact that you are reading this now means that you are probably a little less biased than your peers because you are aware of your own biases, which is a great starting point, and you are probably more curious and open to experience, which is also a great starting point.

So, what can we learn from all the research on biases? Here are four key recommendations:

Cognitive Diversity Must Be Embraced

All this means is that you must learn to accept that there are differences between people, even if you find yourself agreeing with someone who acts, thinks, feels, even speaks differently to you. One good way to begin is to watch a program on the television that you really don't like or listen to a radio show or podcast that you don't agree with. It won't be very comfortable to start with, but it will give you a few good ideas about the differences in people. From that starting point, you should begin to make an effort to get involved with people who don't like your values or who question them.

Empathy Must Be Cultivated

Empathy is one of the oldest topics in the study of psychology and it is defined as a willingness and/or ability to give due consideration to different points of view, to try to understand why other people feel and think the way they do. Plenty of training programs exist that are effective in boosting empathy, programs that have been successful even where the students are total psychopaths. Courses like that are not necessary for you; it is just as easy to practice empathy by yourself and learn to develop it.

Begin by trying to analyze what someone else may be thinking. See if you can understand their attitude or motive. To begin with, your results will be pretty random and way off, but what you are doing is training your mind to put itself in the place of another person. After that, you can try justifying why a person thinks and feels as they do.

Pay attention to the less privileged or disadvantaged; keep in mind that they may have come from a disadvantaged background and may not have had the luck or success that you have had. That doesn't mean that they are not talented, interesting, or that they don't work as hard as you do. Put yourself in their shoes; how would you feel? Think about what it must be like to be held back because you are different in some way.

Doing exercises like these are an easy way of helping you to get into empathic thinking, leading to more tolerance and less bias.

Your Biases Must Be Explicit

Determine your biases, and be honest with yourself. To deal with a bias, you must be certain that it exists and that you are aware of it. The best way is to take the Implicit Association test—it may not be perfect but it will give you a starting point from which you can identify hidden biases, those that you may not have known you had.

Once again, this won't stop you from being biased, but it does highlight the implicit and explicit biases. If you know that you are a racist or a sexist, and you are proud of being that way, this is not going to solve any problems for you. However, the very fact that you have made it this far through the book likely means that you are not racist or sexist and you have no pride in your biases.

Your Behaviors Must Be Controlled

What it all boils down to is that it doesn't matter what you think of or feel about others deep down. What really matters is your behavior—that is the biggest give-away to others whether you are biased or not; actions always speak louder than words and never more so than here. Nobody can be completely free of bias; what you must do is stop those biases from influencing the way you act.

Here's an example for you. Two people: one is thoroughly prejudiced but behaves, as best they can, in an inclusive and social manner, so much so, that everyone believes them to be a fair person. The second is very open-minded, has no real opinion on stereotypes but their behavior is that of a prejudiced person who speaks derogatorily about others.

You probably think this is a scenario that you are never likely to come across but, believe it or not, it is far more common than you will ever know. In simple terms, it is incredibly easy to be an advocate for something or someone if you don't have to show your actions to back it up. Look at the organ donation system—sure, there are millions of supporters, but how many have actually signed up to it? The environment—millions of people are advocates for saving the environment, but few of them follow that by living a lifestyle that is kind to the environment. Some people are prejudiced against socially disadvantaged groups but don't show it, while others are very open about their prejudices. That's life; it's the way we are.

When it comes down to it, we cannot live a life entirely free of bias, but we can learn to put ourselves in other people's shoes. When you can do that, you can question your biases and do something about stopping them from having an influence over how you think and act.

SECTION 3: Tools for the Mind

Cognitive Dissonance: The Power of Belief and How to Overcome It

In Part 3, we will go over actions, the things you can do to train your mind to be a better, less prejudiced thinker. We have a lot to cover here, but you do not need to do everything. You're infinitely better than most people, even if you only implement one of the methods that I will show you here.

Cognitive dissonance is simply the discomfort you experience on the inside that is caused when there is a conflict between your actions and behaviors, or beliefs and new information. For example, if you are a vegetarian and strictly do not eat meat, but you are forced to kill a rabbit and eat it because you are trying to avoid starvation in a life or death situation. Your longstanding belief compels you to stick to your vegetarian lifestyle, but the current situation forces you to either kill or perish. With that said, why do we experience cognitive dissonance?

We experience cognitive dissonance because our mind loves consistency. We all follow some sort of routine, which is a series of actions that occur at a certain time. For example, when you wake up in the morning, you will go to the toilet, brush your teeth, take a shower, get dressed, have breakfast, and go to work. This is a typical morning routine for many people, and we do this almost unconsciously. Our brain loves this sort of thing because it can streamline all actions to make them feel almost automatic. Even when you fold your arms, you always fold them a certain way, either the right tucked under the left or vice versa. If you try to do the opposite, you will feel strange.

We want consistency in our lives, and the lack thereof creates cognitive dissonance. Consistency here applies to our attitudes, habits, and view of the world at large. Whenever something happens that challenges that consistency, you will feel uncomfortable, and you will feel the urge to either reduce or eliminate the dissonance.

Psychologist Leon Festinger proposed a theory on cognitive dissonance. He suggested that we all strive toward internal consistency. It is not just a conscious goal, either. Achieving internal consistency is a psychological need. We all have the need to ensure that our beliefs and behavior align with each other. Inconsistency or conflicts between those two create an internal disharmony that we are programmed to avoid.

According to Festinger's 1957 book called *A Theory of Cognitive Dissonance*, he explained that one could understand cognitive dissonance as a condition that compels the subject to perform activities that reduce this dissonance. He compared it to how hunger compels us to eat to reduce hunger. Of course, cognitive dissonance is a much more powerful motivation, but it is basically that.

Influential Factors

Cognitive dissonance and the severity that people experience this dissonance will depend on some different factors, such as how highly they valued their said challenged belief and how inconsistent their belief is compared to their actions. Many factors may influence the overall strength of cognitive dissonance, including:

• If the challenged cognition is personal—such as belief in oneself—then the severity of the dissonance will be strong. The more personal it is, the stronger the dissonance becomes.

- The importance of cognition also plays a huge role. Other than personal beliefs, how much you value the cognition influences the strength of the dissonance when it occurs.
- The ratio that exists between consonant thoughts and dissonant thoughts. So, the more thoughts that are challenged, the stronger the dissonance is.
- The stronger the dissonance, the more a person feels the urge to remove uncomfortable feelings.
- Since cognitive dissonance compels us to take action to eliminate it, it can influence the way we act and behave in powerful ways.

Examples

Because cognitive dissonance happens when our beliefs and actions are conflicted, or our beliefs are challenged in some way, it can happen when we least expect it, and in any part of our lives. However, the effects are likely to be more significant when there is a strong conflict between behavior and those beliefs that we see as critical to self-identity.

For instance, cognitive dissonance can occur in the purchasing decisions that we make regularly. Take the electric car, for example. One would assume that switching to an electric car would be environmentally beneficial until they realize that the production of the electric car is just as bad for the environment.

In this case, we can see the conflict clearly. The person wants to contribute to the preservation of the environment by switching to an electric car but then finds out that the car may not be as environmentally friendly as they have been led to believe. However, in the long term, it will still cause less emissions into the atmosphere, but they feel guilt over the pollution from its production.

A dissonance occurs, and to reduce it, that person can either get rid of the car and take public transportation, or reduce their emphasis on environmental responsibility. So, as you can see, there are not many choices here when dissonance occurs between belief and action. Either remove the object that causes the dissonance or the belief.

Many of us are confident in our decision-making abilities, and there is also the tendency among humans to overestimate our abilities. In this case, if you made a bad purchase, then it will conflict with your self-belief, therefore causing cognitive dissonance.

Here, Festinger provided an example in his book on how a person might deal with cognitive dissonance when there is a conflict between behavior and health. You might have heard of this, but some people insist on smoking even though they know full well that smoking is unhealthy. In this case, the conflict is between the fact that smoking is bad and the contradicting behavior (smoking).

Therefore, smokers have two options to deal with the dissonance. They can quit smoking, or they can change their belief in the information they received. Some people go for the first option, which is the right one, whereas others opt to place a higher value on smoking than they do on their own health. The people in the second group do not reject the information. They acknowledge that smoking is unhealthy, but they believe that the chemical-induced pleasure they get from smoking is worth it.

There is a third option, and that is to decrease the drawbacks. In our example, the smoker may decide not to believe in the fact that smoking is unhealthy. They tell themselves that what they have heard about smoking so far is biased, so they may do their own research to find studies to prove that smoking is not unhealthy to counteract the new information that contradicts their belief. Alternatively, they may use superficial reasons to convince themselves to continue their behavior. In this case, they may tell themselves that they can't possibly avoid all potential risks out there, so there's no point in avoiding this one.

The smokers may also try to convince themselves that they will gain weight if they stop smoking, which is often true based on numerous studies. The thing is that stopping smoking will only cause you to gain a couple of pounds. There are cases in which people gain much more than that, but the chance is very rare. What the smoker sees is not the insignificant consequence of gaining a few kilos, but rather the fact that they gain weight, and that is a health risk associated with weight gain. So, smokers convince themselves that smoking is not at all bad considering that quitting smoking would cause weight gain.

Common Reaction to Cognitive Dissonance

People feel compelled to reduce cognitive dissonance depending on the severity. There are three common responses that they will display:

• **Shift Focus:** here, the person simply focusses on the supportive beliefs, thus outweighing the discomfort caused by the dissonance. For example, those who feel strongly about the environment may experience extreme cognitive dissonance when they drive a car that burns lots of fuel very quickly. In this case, they may choose to do their own research to find out whether they are contributing to the detriment of the environment. They find out the facts that verify their actions, therefore reducing the discomfort.

• **Reduce Importance:** in the second scenario, let's say that Steve leads a healthy lifestyle, but he works at the office that requires him to sit for eight hours a day, which is unhealthy. The dissonance then occurs when he realizes that sitting for too long is associated with various health problems. He might not be able to request a standing desk, nor can he work by sitting and standing up intermittently. So, his only option is to find ways to justify his behavior, which he can do in many ways, since he can cover up the dissonant action with other activities that support the conflicting belief. Steve may decide to stick to his healthy lifestyle or continue to incorporate more healthy habits to compensate for the conflict.

• **Change the Belief:** finally, you can also choose to change the conflicting belief, so that it aligns with your behavior. This is considered to be the best way to deal with cognitive dissonance if the conflicting belief is a limiting belief. However, changing one's belief is difficult, especially if that belief has to do with deeply ingrained values such as religion.

How Does It Feel to Have Cognitive Dissonance?

Every person has their own levels of tolerance for cognitive dissonance, and, for that reason, it cannot be objectively measured. Some will only experience a mild level of discomfort, a gut feeling that something is wrong, but not severe enough to bring about a sense of urgency or cause any major problems for them. Some will want to make changes to remove that discomfort straight away, and that's no bad thing.

However, the worst-case is a powerful dissonance that causes anxiety, more so when it is affecting a deep value or belief, like morality or religion. For example, growing up in a strict religion that teaches you that having sex before you get married is sinful; if you then get involved in a sexual relationship before you are married, you are likely to feel a strong cognitive dissonance.

To a certain extent, one community affected by cognitive dissonance is the LGBT+ community, although things are not as bad as they used to be. If, for example, you were taught that it was wrong to have sexual feelings about a person of the same sex, you may begin to experience strong feelings of embarrassment, guilt, anger, or shame if you do, and that comes from cognitive dissonance. If it is strong enough, you might even begin to believe that you are immoral, a degenerate even, and you could start to hate yourself until you can resolve the dissonance.

Three Ways to Decrease Cognitive Dissonance

Cognitive dissonance is peppered throughout our lives; some of it is tolerable while some of it is powerful—the latter makes us want to make immediate changes. It is almost impossible to achieve consistency throughout our lives because all that we do and believe will be challenged at some point, requiring changes to be made. According to experts, there are three ways that we can all decrease cognitive dissonance:

- **Change How You Behave:** cognitive dissonance rears its head when your actions and beliefs are in conflict. One way of decreasing dissonance is to change the belief or action that caused it. For example, if you drink and drive regularly, the way to decrease dissonance is to stop—stop drinking altogether or stop driving when you drink—and teach yourself that it is not okay to drive when under the influence. By doing this, actions and beliefs are harmonized, and dissonance is eliminated or at least significantly decreased.

- **Change Your Beliefs:** the human brain creates a lens, and it is through this that our reality is perceived. Your reality may be different from those around you, and reality perception is constantly being altered to relieve dissonant feelings. What that means is that the human mind will filter out anything that doesn't fit with its beliefs, so dissonance is only experienced when it is completely unavoidable. For example, smokers may constantly look for information about the link between smoking and cancer, choosing to believe the research that says there is no real link. This is biased behavior, but smokers continue to do this as a way of reducing dissonance and carrying on as before.

- **Justifying Your Behavior and Beliefs:** this is never a good idea when those beliefs and behaviors can potentially harm others, and when "bad" behavior is in conflict with a "good" belief. Let's take the person who just loves to spend money; they may be continually convincing themselves that they can't take the money with them when they die, so they may as well spend it, or, simply, that money is earned to be spent. Another example would be the person who gets involved in something risky; they may justify this by saying that life is there for the living, and that you just don't know when your time is up. We could flip things around, say that the action is "good," and the belief is "bad"—there would still be cognitive dissonance, but you would be opening up the potential to change the bad belief.

Cognitive Dissonance and Emotionally Draining Relationships

We have all been involved with or know someone who is with a person who drains energy, known as an "energy vampire." These people use abusive tactics, like physical and emotional abuse, intimidating behavior, sexual abuse, social isolation, economic abuse, and many more damaging behaviors, just to keep control over the victim. The threat of abuse is always hanging over the victim, and, as time goes on, it gets worse.

Victims tend to ignore gut feelings, not believing in them when it comes to these kinds of relationships. Deep down, they know it's all wrong; they know that they are the victim in an abusive relationship, but they continue to stay, living in fear of what could happen, in the mistaken hope that things will get better.

This causes a deep cognitive dissonance because the victim wants to believe that everything will be okay, while knowing that it won't. They want to believe that if they show their partner love and attention, he or she will change. The reality is very different, because "energy vampires" have no idea what love is. Their idea of love is to continue the abuse; shaming, criticizing, and punishing their partner.

The main defense mechanism of anyone caught in such a relationship is to do whatever they can to decrease the dissonance. There are those three ways we talked about earlier, but these are the least resistive methods and will do nothing to ease things for the victim. Nothing is going to change, and they won't feel any safer.

A victim of this type of relationship may, for example, lie: convincing themselves that their partner really does love them, as a way of justifying what is happening. They tell themselves that when a good thing happens, everything will change for the better, but every time they are subjected to more abuse, the dissonance just becomes stronger.

There is a good reason why a victim should get out as quickly as possible—changes in the brain. The longer you live with cognitive dissonance, the more likely it is your brain will change, similar to how it does with PTSD. Physical symptoms may manifest themselves as autoimmune diseases, and victims may even experience certain brain disorders. Once that happens, the victim is no longer able to think properly, they cannot see a way out, and things will not change until they learn to have trust in themselves once more. There are ways that this kind of situation can be fixed, though, using therapies such as Tapping or Eye Movement Desensitization and Reprocessing (EMDR) therapy.

How to Decrease Dissonance Following a Relationship with an Energy Vampire

If you have been caught in a relationship with an energy vampire, it will take more than just reduction techniques to build you back up. Obviously, the first step is to remove yourself from the relationship. Then you can begin the process of recovery.

Aside from the methods mentioned above, there is one more way to deal with cognitive dissonance after this kind of relationship. The victim must get some validation for the situation—therapy with a professional, chatting to a friend, writing it all down, and so on.

Neuroplasticity: Change Your Limiting Beliefs Now

As the name suggests, neuroplasticity is a term used to describe the flexibility of the mind. More accurately, it is the ability of the mind to be molded, like plastic, based on thoughts and behavior. Indeed, it does not matter how old you are; your mind can still be changed for the better. But before we dive too deeply into this, let's start from the beginning.

How Beliefs Are Formed and How to Change Them

Everyone is different. That fact has already been established. No two bodies are identical, and no two individuals have exactly the same life experiences, thinking patterns, and personalities. The way our bodies function is also not exactly identical either. In the diet and lifestyle world, it has been proven that two people will get different results from the same diet even if they follow it to the letter. This difference is also present in our psyche. We each have a belief set that shapes our individual lives.

I've probably mentioned and will mention this several times, but it is worth stressing the fact that we perceive the world through a lens constructed by our beliefs. This influences how we see ourselves and everything around us. Therefore, our beliefs have a powerful influence on our actions and emotions. As a result, our success and happiness also depend on our beliefs. This is exactly why successful people always tell us to believe in ourselves if we want to be successful. There is no precise recipe for success other than self-belief.

What is a Belief?

So, with that said and done, what exactly is a "belief?" Simply put, a belief is something that we think is true. Pay attention here because the keyword here is "think." Just because we think something is true does not make it true.

Therefore, belief is anything we assume is true, and we use it to help us understand the world, to navigate it. Think of it as a system to help us operate in this world. It can even save our lives, because a belief can influence what we do and feel. Since belief is a safety mechanism, we are naturally inclined to protect and preserve our beliefs once this system is formed.

Our beliefs work at the subconscious level, much like the autopilot system in a self-driving car, for example. When you form a belief and give it enough time to become reinforced, you start to take it for granted and never question whether your beliefs are accurate or not.

We all have different sets of beliefs, meaning that we all have different perceptions of reality. Two people can disagree quite passionately about a particular subject, leading to conflict, all because of a difference in beliefs. Some good examples include politics, traditionalism and modernism, death sentences, abortion, et cetera.

On a more personal level, our beliefs also change how we see challenges or any problems. Some see them as a setback and another reason to give up, whereas others see them as a learning opportunity and a stepping-stone to success.

How Are Beliefs Formed?

Have you ever wondered why children need to go to school and receive education early on when they could probably do better when they are adults? To help you understand why, think of our minds in this way: when we arrive in this world, our minds are like blank canvases or a wet piece of clay. We start with a clean slate that has limitless possibilities. That means that when we were kids, we had no preconceived beliefs. What we had were curiosity and the powers of observation.

Since children know so little about the world, the only way they can learn is from others around them. That means learning from their parents, teachers, friends, and other people they encounter. So, your core beliefs are pretty much formed by external factors that are well outside of your control.

From this, we can identify two main sources of beliefs. The first is the acceptance of what others tell us to be facts, which is often what children do. But as we grow older, another factor comes into play that arguably has a more powerful influence on our beliefs, and that is our past experiences.

Here's an example of how beliefs are formed. Suppose that during one Thanksgiving dinner, you (as a kid) didn't eat all of your dinner because you already felt full. It could be because the serving size was too big or you had too many cookies before the meal, but the cause didn't matter—what mattered then was the fact that your parents saw that you still had some food left, and they reprimanded you for it. They may have told you that good children eat everything on their plates or they pointed out the fact that the world is full of starving children, and you not finishing the food meant that you were ungrateful. Although the actual message that your parents may have wanted to tell you was that one should never be wasteful, the way that they phrased this lesson influenced your beliefs in more ways than one.

At that point, if we take what our parents said to heart and believe that it is true, then they have planted a seed of belief that will manifest itself. In this case, that means you will grow up believing that good children should eat every last bit of food that they are served, no matter how much or little there is. This could either lead to malnutrition or overeating, more so in the latter case if you have a grandmother, for example, who is very generous with her portion sizes. Another belief formed here is that we think disagreeing with our parents would mean that we were being "ungrateful," which is a really powerful label for children. All of these beliefs would have been further reinforced whenever we did not finish our food and got reprimanded for it.

Having something as personal as our core beliefs being shaped by outside factors may seem like a bad idea but, to be fair, we need to learn from others around us. Just like every other aspect of our lives, we have to start somewhere. It does not matter so much about what beliefs we've formed so far, because we could not stop them from being formed in the past. What matters is what we can do right now about it. What is learned can be unlearned, and the same applies here. You can change your beliefs.

But our minds still undergo further changes when we leave home and attend schools and meet more people. For one, the teachers will also tell you what they think is true and right. Again, since we have no prior experience in life, at least other than what our parents—or parental figures—have already told us, we also accept what our teachers tell us to be true.

For example, suppose that you didn't do very well in math (partly because the teacher did not do a good job teaching it), your teacher may tell you that you are bad at math or you are lazy. Then, you start to believe what the teacher has told you, especially when they do it several times. Eventually, you come to believe that you are actually bad at math, or you truly believe that you are lazy, even though that is false.

When you are at school, you are subject to more influence from your peers and classmates, because you spend more time with them than your teachers. Suppose they decide to bully you by calling you nasty names or even going as far as being physically abusive; you may feel that whatever they call you is true, and you will feel defenseless.

So, the moment that we accept that something is a fact, a belief is formed, and it is ingrained into the subconscious mind. When that happens, it will be difficult to remove that belief because it is not something that you can just consciously reach into. While you can reason with your conscious mind to discern truth from falsehood, the subconscious mind cannot be reasoned with. It takes our beliefs and uses them as a reference to form our perception of the world and automate our responses.

How Our Beliefs Affect Our Behavior, Emotions, and Thoughts

Here's an example that we can all relate to. I'm certain that you have crossed roads multiple times in your life. Take a moment now and think of how you act when you need to get across a busy road. For one, you may notice that you follow a set of behaviors automatically. You first look each way to ensure the road is clear for you to walk across. Sometimes, you might even run across just to get to the other side quicker. If you see a car coming your way when you are crossing the street, you may feel tense. Just crossing the street alone, regardless of the traffic, can be anxiety-inducing for many people. Whatever and however you do it, the chances are that you do it consistently. You have the brain to thank for automating the entire process.

What I want to point out is not how one should cross the road, but rather how the automated system in our brain is created. You see, the way you cross the street is the product of only one of countless other beliefs. All of these combined create a complex system of automatic responses and thoughts. Some of the beliefs are true and useful, and others are harmful, as they are not based on facts.

When a belief is recently developed, it is easy to change it because it hasn't spent enough time in our minds. However, when a belief has been reinforced over and over, across several years, it becomes so deeply rooted that we simply fail to perceive the reality that contradicts that belief. Our mind simply throws away all reason and only looks for the information that validates and reinforces our belief to avoid cognitive dissonance. Why does the mind do that?

You see, humans are lazy creatures. We want things to be as easy as possible, and our mind is like that as well. It always goes on the path of least resistance. In this case, one can either change the longstanding-belief or change how information is perceived. The easiest thing to do would be to change how one interprets information.

That means it does not really matter how the information is presented. No matter how convincing it looks, if it is a direct contradiction to your longstanding belief in the subconscious mind, you won't acknowledge a single word. Plus, since our beliefs change how we see the world, and our thoughts, actions, and emotions are our response to the world, that means that our beliefs also influence them.

For example, let's say that you believe that dogs are dangerous. Maybe your parents told you that, or you have been horribly maimed in the past by the neighbor's pit bull. As a result, you have a powerful belief in the dangers of these lovely mutts and would do everything in your power to avoid contact with them. This impulse causes your mind to develop various automatic responses to anything related to dogs.

You might feel anxious, and your body tenses up when you even sense the presence of a dog because you see it as an impending danger. If you see one growling and adopting an aggressive stance, then you'll see it as a threat. You may recall the time when you got bitten or remember your parent's warning, and you will feel threatened.

Because you develop the belief that dogs are aggressive and dangerous creatures, you won't even notice a friendly dog. You will still see that pup as a threat, and you will respond accordingly. It's almost as if we see the world through a lens with filters created by the beliefs ingrained in our subconscious minds.

As I've mentioned before, beliefs may be both beneficial and limiting. When you start to question your own beliefs, you will see which is which. Negative or limiting beliefs stop us from reaching our full potential. However, positive or empowering beliefs are based on facts and logic. They let us remain resilient and thrive in the face of hardship.

In a way, our beliefs shape our view of reality. The thing is that not many people notice that because our beliefs are so obscure that we do not take time out to scrutinize our sense of reality. Since our beliefs change our view of reality, thoughts, and behaviors, they also influence how successful we can be in life. One person may see a problem as a challenge to overcome, whereas another may see it as a dead-end, all because of their beliefs. You don't even need to look far to find such examples. You might even know some of those people personally, those who managed to overcome all odds and those who gave up at the slightest hint of inconvenience, even though they had all the resources and ability they needed to overcome the problem.

These are just a few of the ways that one situation is viewed differently by different people. Bear in mind that we all try to do whatever we can to reinforce our beliefs, to validate them, because it is so much easier to wrongly interpret something than it is to change what we believe in. Everyone feels, thinks, and acts in a way that they see as appropriate. We could even go so far as to say that strong beliefs will create self-fulfillment.

Now we understand the importance of beliefs; we need to look a little closer at them. It's great when you have all "good" beliefs, but if you can identify your beliefs and eliminate the limiting ones from your subconscious, you will go a long way. It isn't going to be easy, but then nothing worth having is. After all, nobody wants to live their life confined by beliefs that only make them unhappy, which stops them from achieving their potential.

Identifying Negative or Limiting Beliefs

The first step to change is not to out-right challenge your limiting beliefs. You want to first discern the good from the bad. This will take some time because you will have many beliefs to analyze. I recommend spending some time alone at home on the weekend and asking yourself a bunch of questions to identify limiting beliefs. It will take a long time and require a lot of effort. It won't be comfortable for you either, if you do it right.

Nonetheless, I want to point out again that finding limiting beliefs and replacing them with empowering ones will be worth the trouble. You will know this the moment you manage to uproot a limiting belief and replace it with an empowering belief. It is a life-changing experience.

So, try to find some time alone in a place you won't be disturbed. Have a pen and a notebook ready. Then, ask yourself a lot of questions. Here are a few to get you started:

- "What are the things that I want, but fail to get?"
- "What do I want to improve, but I never get the result I want?"
- "What areas of my life do I feel incompetent about?"

These are only a few questions that you can ask yourself. It will be a soul-searching journey, so you want to take your time with this one. The idea is that you identify what areas in life you are falling behind with, how and why that happened, and you might find the limiting belief behind it all. These questions may look simply, but these will be some of the most difficult ones you will ever ask yourself, as they should be. You won't get the real answer immediately, and it will take a lot of time and brutal honesty. The latter is definitely going to be difficult for you, as it requires you to accept the reality of your beliefs, and this may cause cognitive dissonance. Since we're talking about deeply rooted beliefs, the dissonance will be strong. No matter how strong it is, you might want to develop another belief by telling yourself that if you make the change and endure the pain, it will be worth your efforts.

Replacing Limiting Beliefs

Once all your limiting beliefs have been identified, you can begin to eliminate them and replace them with empowering beliefs. It isn't enough just to eliminate the limiting ones from your life; you need to develop the most empowering beliefs that you can. None of this will be easy; your brain and mind are no longer a clean slate, and changing everything you thought you believed in will be hard.

Since our brain loves consistency, we can use that to our advantage. To change your beliefs, you will need consistency and time, lots of it. The task itself is simple. Anyone can do that, but your success relies on whether you can stick to it. Take it as slowly as you need to—as long as you can stick to it consistently. Consistency is what is important here. There is no need to rush something as delicate as this.

Just like anything man-made, we can unlearn limiting beliefs and form empowering ones. So, here are the things you need to do:

1. Choose one limiting belief; think hard about how it has worked against you previously. In doing so, you are establishing the fact that you have good reasons to want to remove it. The best way to do this is by isolating it by contrasting it with all the empowering beliefs you have. It will create a dissonance, but your mind will be convinced that the best way to eliminate the dissonance is by removing the limiting belief. For example, suppose that you have trust issues. You are convinced that everyone is out there trying to exploit you. Ask yourself why you have this belief. Maybe you had a terrible break-up because your spouse cheated on you. Maybe you never really have any friends. Perhaps you simply believe that trusting someone is a sign of weakness since you can get hurt when they are not honest with you. Then, look at how this belief has harmed you. Maybe no one at work really likes you. You live mostly in isolation, and you feel lonely. Perhaps you even feel guilty for pushing away the people that genuinely care about you.

2. Look for the evidence proving that a belief is not true; when you can accept that the belief is harming your life, you can then reinforce this fact, and that a particular limiting belief is not good for you. To do this, you need to find more evidence to convince yourself. Going back to the distrust example we used before, you might think back to when a person you were dating was very honest with you about something, something that caused discomfort and damaged your relationship. Perhaps you can think of times when you were at school, and a group of kids you didn't know allowed you to sit with them at lunch. And, no doubt, you can think of a time when you took a chance on trusting a person and it worked out for you, perhaps of a good friend you had in the past who never lied to you and didn't, at any time, ever fail you. Basically, find evidence from your past experience and acknowledge that all of those events happened. Allow them to sink in to the point where you accept and have been convinced that the limiting belief is not true. I recommend spending as much time as you need on the first two steps here because you can still receive many benefits by just removing limiting beliefs alone. You don't have to focus on incorporating empowering beliefs if you do not want to. One less negative and limiting belief is an amazing improvement already.

3. **The next step is to start planting the seed of an empowering belief;** going back to the last example, try telling yourself that it's only a small minority of people that are dishonest, and you know that from your own experiences. By now, you have sufficient evidence for this belief to be established, and by doing so, you can release the limiting belief, admit that it wasn't true, acknowledge the fact that it has just been getting in your way all this time, and move on—begin believing that most people are naturally honest.

4. **Finally, it's a matter of reinforcing the empowering belief;** to do this, you must constantly remind yourself of the new empowering belief. This is not going to be easy, given how long you have had the old limiting beliefs. Do not go into this with the expectation that the empowering belief will just magically embed itself in your subconscious straight away. It's going to take time, and it's going to take consistency, especially where limiting beliefs have long been ingrained in you. The recommendation is this—whenever you can, remind yourself that you have a new belief; the more you do it, the more that new belief will become embedded and reinforced. And the more reinforced it is, the more empowering it will be. Try to remind yourself every morning and every night if you can.

Our belief systems are very powerful because they influence every aspect of our lives, including how we think, feel, and act. Unfortunately, something this important is so obscure that many people fail to see it. People take their beliefs for granted and believe that whatever it is they believe in to be facts, which is often not the case. When we take the time and effort to examine our own beliefs closely, we can then start to root out the limiting beliefs that stop us from living the best life we can live. From there, we can start to replace those limiting thoughts with the ones that will empower us in ways that we could never imagine.

Taking Advantage of Neuroplasticity

Take a moment now and observe—how do you converse with yourself? How would you describe your life to others? Do you fault-find in just about every aspect of your life? Now think about the language you use when you talk to others, or talk about them—is it the same as you do about you and your own life?

We go through our days without conscious observation of our thoughts. The world is busy; we are busy; we are simply too bogged down with other things that we just don't have time to listen to our own minds. When we do stop and take time to listen, we are surprised, perhaps even shocked at how much negativity we use when we talk to ourselves. That negativity may overwhelm you and leave you feeling like you have no power over your mind; no power over the direction your mind wants to take you in.

We have always had the belief that our brains were hard-wired, and there was no way of changing them. Wasn't everyone born with an inherited trait that made them special and gifted in some way? Now we know that is not true and that our brains are constantly changing.

Just one thought has the potential to determine how our brain is structured. The more compassionate you are when you talk with yourself, the easier you find it to pick yourself up and carry on when you fail at something.

We've all heard Gandhi's quote: "Your beliefs become your thoughts, your thoughts become your words, your words become your actions, your actions become your habits, your habits become your values, and your values become your destiny."

Neuroplasticity is an emerging scientific field. Put simply, neuroplasticity is how the brain can mold itself into different shapes, much like plastic can be molded. It is how the brain forms neural connections so it can reorganize itself. In this way, we know that the brain can be changed and, although it takes time, we know that we can teach it new tricks.

Over time, our understanding of neuroplasticity has changed, bringing about a new treatment for dyslexia, cancer prevention, injury, and stroke victims. But it doesn't just work in medical and scientific fields; we can also apply what we know about it to every part of our lives, and the process of that is simple.

The changes happen in all parts of our brains, including the amygdala and the cingulate cortex but, for those of you that are not neuroscientists, you don't really need to understand how the brain is affected by those changes. Medical and scientific names are irrelevant; all that matters is how simple it all is.

So far, we've only touched on the basics of the human brain; it is an incredibly complex machine, and the details about how the changes happen are also complex. The most important thing is that you can change your brain by using your mind.

Bear in mind that all these changes mean the human brain is rewiring itself all the time. Sometimes those wires will be all over the place; other times, it will reinforce the positive and not the negative thoughts. Evolution has meant that our brains have developed a bad habit—we cling to negativity, mostly for survival, rather than discarding it. Rewiring your brain requires you to do it all yourself by controlling your own mind.

When you were younger, somebody did all of your thinking for you, leaving you with no choice. Now that you are an adult you have to make your own choices. All that negative self-talk has already done a number on your brain, and it's guided you down your life path so far—now you need to stop it, rebuild that path in another, more positive direction.

Ground-breaking research, a combination of Eastern practices and Western science, was carried out by Harvard Medical School and the University of Wisconsin. The research was done to see what power the mind has over shaping the brain.

Professor Richard Davidson wanted to look at how meditation affected the brain; the fourteenth Dalai Lama provided him with twelve Tibetan Buddhists with a combined amount of over 10,000 meditation hours between them. In Buddhism, it is believed that compassion and meditation can only change someone for the better, but those are just two of many Buddhist practices. This research was the first time that we had been able to study how meditation affected us; all we knew was that it changed something, but we didn't know what. The results of the study suggested that meditation can change the way the brain is structured, but not only that, it can change how it functions too. It was seen that the subjects had gamma wave activity in their brains that was more powerful than anything ever seen before.

Gamma brain activity governs our cognitive functioning, learning, memory, consciousness, perception, etc., meaning that changes are best introduced once the gamma brain activity increases. It takes practice to increase activity in that area, but you don't have to become a monk to do so. Simple mindfulness practices such as meditation are powerful enough to change the way the brain is structured, particularly in the areas connected with compassion and awareness.

With that said, you can induce positive changes in your brain by undoing the faulty configurations that have plagued you for so long. Consider doing the following:

Awareness

As with anything in life, to make a change, you must recognize your current situation and the need to make that change. In this case, to make positive changes in the brain, one must recognize the problems in there first. So, learn to recognize negative thoughts. This is fairly simple.

Start by listening to the way you talk to yourself and ask yourself how you would feel if someone else were to tell you the same thing. If you think that it is unacceptable for someone to tell you the things you tell yourself, then the chances are that you are too hard on yourself.

Other than that, I recommend you write down the negative thoughts on a notepad and go over it once a week. Do this for a month, and you should have a fairly extensive list of negative self-talk. When you look at the list, try to see if you can identify certain patterns that may lead to a bigger underlying problem. Maybe you'll see that your negative self-talk comes from your deteriorating relationship, lack of career advancement, et cetera.

Whatever you do, never judge your own negative thoughts. Just recognize that you have negative thoughts. Why? Because you want to learn to cut yourself some slack as well. When you judge your negative self-talk, you are partially judging and blaming yourself, and that is not the path to self-compassion. Acknowledge that you have been talking to yourself in a bad way, but forgive yourself and focus your energy on improving yourself instead.

When you are going about your daily life, watch the way that you converse with yourself. If you start thinking negatively, stop; breathe deeply, tell yourself that you will extend the same compassion to yourself that you do to others. In short, be a compassionate observer of your own mind without judgment.

Find the Silver Lining

Simply put, find something good out of the bad situation you find yourself in. We have a bad habit when it comes to how we see problems. We all have them; maybe it's the bad economy and massive layoffs; a difficult boss; or that your company's culture is toxic. Maybe it's your mean and unsupportive family; or you don't have enough resources, education, experience, or finances to get what you want. The list goes on and on.

Many people don't know that what is really holding them back isn't the problem itself. It's how they see their problems and the story they tell themselves about them. The things that you tell yourself may just be excuses to keep you inside your comfort zone. So, be honest with yourself and see problems as they are, but not worse than they are. Life is full of problems, but instead of seeing them as obstacles, see them as stepping stones.

Morning Routine

First, let us start with the morning routine. What is yours like? Does it consist of you waking up to the blaring alarm, feeling groggy, and cursing yourself for staying up late so you could watch "Just one more" episode of the latest and hottest Netflix series? Is it all about coffee and email and everyone else's needs first? If so, then you need to freshen up your morning. You want to have a morning with intention and direction instead of the chaos and distractions we all are too familiar with.

You need to have a consistent morning routine, so you are free from distractions, feel energetic, are present in the moment and enjoy life—while maintaining that beautiful creative flow and making good life decisions.

Again, you want to start small. You don't have to overhaul your morning routine completely. So, do the following small things in the morning:

1. No more excuses. We all say that we're not a morning person and so it's natural that your morning is always a mess. I'll tell you this now: no one is born a morning person. It takes a conscious effort to establish a morning routine and remain consistent with it. So, start your morning routine whenever your morning starts.

2. Gratitude stretch. I understand that this sounds like a bit of a "stretch"—pardon the pun. But when you wake up, you want to stretch your muscles to let them know that it is time to get busy again. Don't forget to stretch your abs because the arms and legs aren't enough. While you are at it, try to come up with three things you are grateful for and say them to yourself.

3. Ignore the notifications. Just ignore those for now to create a little haven from the digital world for the first waking hour. You want your morning to be stress-free and without distractions. So that means not going online or checking your phone for any messages if you can help it. You don't want to get distracted with Facebook updates or become stressed when you check the emails from your boss. You want to start the day on your own terms. If you really need to catch up and get ready for the day ahead, do it at the last moment, so you know what to expect before you go to work. This brings us to the fourth step.

4. Go outside. Get out there, really. You want to start your day with fresh air in your lungs and sunshine on your face. If possible, I recommend you do more than just standing outside on your porch or balcony to enjoy the view. That is fine, but if you can get out and have a short walk around the neighborhood, that is even better.

5. Go inside. After you have soaked in the beauty and energy of the morning, head inside and do something more for your mind. I'm talking about reflection, meditation, praying, or simply just sit and be in the present moment. Spend a few minutes here and pay attention to how you are feeling. We all have asked other people how they are, but so few of us have stopped and asked ourselves how we are. Your body and heart will tell you, and this can lead to more questions and answers. Taking the time to ask yourself these questions can be relieving in itself. Just pay attention to your body and mind.

6. Create a morning "not-to-do" list. This is a reverse concept of a to-do list. You might have a better idea of what you want to do in the morning by making it clear what you *don't* want to do. These are the things that don't add value to your morning, so spend some time figuring out what they are. Things such as social media and YouTube are definitely on the list.

7. Show up. Even if you cannot follow through with all of these recommendations, I suggest that you at least do something during your morning routine. That may be doing yoga for only five minutes or stretching in your bedroom, whatever you would like to do. Try to stick to a routine for at least a week. Start sorting out your morning plan and stick to it, but do it at your own pace.

Meditation

Meditation should be part of your morning or evening routine. It serves as a tool to calm your mind. Think of meditation as a transitional period, from a relaxed to an alert state at the start of the day, and vice versa at the end of the day. Meditation allows your body and mind to unwind and prepare for sleep. In the end, you will have a clearer mind, a more restful sleep, and other benefits. In this case, it can also be a tool to fight sugar cravings.

Meditation has many forms, but the most popular one is guided meditation because it is beginner-friendly. If you can, I recommend the traditional meditation in which no tools are needed. All you need is a quiet and open space free from distraction. A meditation bench or mat is unnecessary unless you have back pain. Other props are completely unnecessary.

Once you have found that perfect meditation space, simply sit down on the floor in a meditation pose or sit on a chair with your back straight, make sure that your back is not leaning against the wall or the backrest. The idea here is to get you to practice mindfulness and concentration at the same time.

Once you get in your position, simply close your eyes and start breathing from your diaphragm. This is the best way of breathing as you can fully fill your lungs with air as you breathe in. Your stomach should rise as you breathe in. If your shoulders or chest move, then you are breathing from the chest, which is shallow breathing and is an incorrect way to breathe.

As you breathe, focus on your own breathing, which practices concentration. At the same time, make sure you are aware of your own thoughts and posture, which is a mindfulness practice. If your mind starts to wander, gently guide your mind back to your own breathing. If you start to slouch, straighten your back.

If you use guided meditation, you will be given instructions throughout the meditation process. If you follow the traditional meditation practice, you will need a timer. Your phone will do, so long as you set it to "Do Not Disturb" mode so no one can reach you while you meditate.

If you are new to meditation, I recommend you spend only two minutes for the first one or two weeks. You can then increase it to five, then ten minutes once you are comfortable.

Personally, I have a clock that makes a ticking sound every second. So, I focus on the ticking sound and count it each time. Five seconds to inhale, one-second hold, five seconds exhale, and one-second hold. That means I spend twelve seconds for the whole breathing cycle. If I repeat this cycle ten times, then I get 120 seconds of meditation, which is two minutes.

By following this meditation style, you can do the math and find out exactly how many breathing cycles you need to do based on the time you want to spend in meditation. Five minutes of meditation equals twenty-five breathing cycles. Ten minutes of meditation equals fifty breathing cycles.

At first, it will be difficult, especially for those who lead busy lives and need to think all the time. Meditation should be the last thing you do before you hit the hay and one of the first things you do in the morning. This is what you should be doing to have a calm morning and a restful sleep, but you should do more in order to fight sugar cravings. You can use it to break the behavioral pattern that leads you straight to needing sugar.

Whenever a sugar craving strikes, drop whatever you're doing immediately and do a quick meditation. If you're at home, you should have a meditation spot already. If you're outside or at work, you can just meditate while sitting in your chair. Just put your hands on your knees, close your eyes, and breathe deeply. How long you plan to stay that way depends on the situation, but try to go for five minutes if you can. That's twenty-five breathing cycles. In the end, you should feel the craving subside.

How to Solve Any Problem

What do you do when you have a problem to solve? Do you charge straight at it, or do you sweep it under the rug and hope it goes away? Either of these options is not the best way to solve your problems. Although one should be commended for not shying away from problems and choosing to dive headfirst into the problem, if you do so without prior planning, then you stand a good chance of failing spectacularly.

Some problems do go away if you leave them there for a while, but those problems are most likely the things that you should not concern yourself with anyway. But the problems that persist will cause a lot of harm to your life if you don't address them as soon as possible.

So, what you need is an effective approach to problem-solving that covers all your bases so you can remain organized and on top of your game. What you need is a system to help you think systematically. Here is a 10-step system to enhance your critical thinking and problem-solving skills:

1. Rephrase

First of all, you need to change how you view the problem. To be more precise, you need to use a more positive description of your situation. In fact, the word "problem" carries a negative label. It suggests that something is wrong.

So, instead of calling it a problem, call it a challenge or an opportunity to learn. A positive description of the situation also influences how you view and approach it. Calling it a challenge may even encourage you to come up with creative solutions.

2. Define the Situation Clearly

The last thing you want to do is to put yourself in a situation where you have no clue what is going on and what is at stake. So, ask yourself what exactly is going on and identify the sources of your stress, anxiety, and worry, as well as why they make you feel that way. Make sure to write down your answers and be as precise as possible.

3. Use Critical Thinking

The next step would be to analyze the problem and explore your options. Before you jump straight into it, ask yourself what else is the problem because you may overlook the bigger issue at hand. To verify whether there is something else you need to address, keep asking yourself the same question until you no longer get superficial answers.

Maybe the issue you are experiencing is only the symptom and not the disease, so to speak. The same thing applies to problem-solving. You want to get to the root of the problem.

When you have identified the root cause, take some time to think about how you could approach it. The keyword here is "could," not "should." For now, just brainstorm different solutions because there is almost always more than one solution to a problem. Find out what you can do about it and write down your possible course of action.

4. Define the Ideal Solution

Next, you want to identify your criteria for success, so you know what the best course of action is. The ideal solution should address most, if not all, the criteria for success. To help you figure out what they are, ask yourself the following questions:
- "What are the things that must be addressed?"
- "What problems should the solution address?"
- "What would the ideal outcome be?"

In short, you want to know what conditions you need to meet to consider the problem "solved." You may end up with a long list of conditions, so you want to prioritize which condition you want to address first.

Of course, when you identify the conditions for success, you also define failure, and that is the failure to meet the conditions. This is why most people do not define their success. But this step is necessary because if you want to solve problems properly, you need to know exactly what success looks like to you.

5. Pick the Best Solution

When you define the conditions for success, you should have a clear idea of what solution is best for the problem. The best solution should be the one that checks as many boxes as possible, or all the boxes that matter.

6. Prepare for the Worst

Keep in mind that literally, everything can go wrong, even when you plan meticulously. There are only a finite number of factors that you can control, and you pretty much have to rely on luck in certain areas. So, when you plan a course of action, remember that things can go wrong. Study how things can go wrong. You don't have to analyze all the possible unfavorable outcomes. You just need to be aware of the worst thing that could happen.

Proper planning accounts for what *can* happen, not what *should* happen. So, you want to have a contingency plan ready just in case things go wrong. You may need to make some compromises, but if you cannot accept that, try the next best solution.

7. Measure Your Progress

Next, set up measures based on your decision. This is different from defining success criteria. It's about setting up markers to measure your progress. So, ask yourself the following questions:
- "How will I measure success?"
- "How will I compare the success of this solution against that of another?"

Of course, defining the criteria means that you need something to measure your progress. Think of something that can be easily tracked that relates to your success.

8. Take Complete Responsibility

Take full responsibility for the implementation of the decision. Did you know that many people in this world have had the most creative ideas, but they never materialized? It is because the owner of the ideas is specifically assigned the responsibility for carrying out the decision. When you have a responsibility, you take action; without it, you will not. So, take complete responsibility.

9. Set a Deadline

To claim full responsibility for your solution, you also need to set a deadline to add that bit of pressure to get things done. A decision without a deadline is worthless. If it is a major decision that will take a long time to implement, consider setting a series of short-term deadlines and a schedule for reporting.

Remember what we just discussed about measuring your progress? You can use those as sub-deadlines. With these, you will know immediately if you are on track or if you are falling behind. With this knowledge, you can use your creative thinking to prevent similar problems from occurring in the future.

10. Take Action

Finally, take action. While planning is important, what is more important is taking action. It doesn't matter how great your plan is if you don't put it to use, right? So, get after it. You have already developed a sense of urgency with deadlines. The faster you move in the direction of your goals, the more creative you will be, the more energy you will have, and the more you will learn. Most importantly, you will enhance your capacity further so you can achieve even more in the future.

How to Make Non-Biased Decisions

In most case studies, you are given enough information to make decisions, and the answers are textbook examples of human decision-making at its finest. They always present situations in which all the facts are known, and people in the examples are thinking logically. This is the ideal situation, but the reality is often disappointing.

In our everyday lives, we almost always never have enough information, and we have to make decisions in the face of ambiguity, and we also have to deal with our own emotions in the decision-making process. We have to contend with uncertainty, risks, and biases, all of which require us to keep our emotions in check.

Thankfully much work has been done by psychologists to understand the way we think and find out how we can make better decisions. Before we get into it, we need to make one thing clear first: we do not think the same way for each situation. You may make a snappy, spontaneous decision in one case, but then the next decision you make requires you to stop and think for a bit. To make things simple, let's say that there are two processes: fast and slow thinking (System 1 and 2, respectively). Both of these have their own values and drawbacks.

Thinking Fast and Slow

The following concept is derived from the behavioral economist Daniel Kahneman. He proposes a framework consisting of two cognitive systems:

- **System 1:** rapid-fire and automatic, this thinking system allows us to make quick decisions that require little mental resources. This process is prone to error, but best used for mundane decisions.
- **System 2:** slow but accurate, this thinking system allows us to make more complex decisions at the cost of more mental resources.

Knowing which one to use is crucial. System 1, as mentioned, allows you to make quick decisions based on assumptions, so it is best used when you need to decide on insignificant things such as which shoes you want to wear for the day. It is not ideal when you need to make important decisions, however, because you will be subject to biases. This is where System 2 comes in. System 2 is more resource-demanding, as it requires you to gather information, but you can deliberate on more complex problems. In short, to make the most out of your decision-making capacity, you need to know which system to use.

Simple Rules for Better Decision-Making

In light of all this, here are some tips to enhance your decision-making:

Rest or Sleep on It

If a decision is important, the chances are that you still have some time to think about it. You want to be in the best frame of mind when you make such decisions, after all. So, get some rest so you can focus. In this case, System 2 is best. Important decisions should not be made on a whim, and you don't want to make them when you feel tired and stressed out.

Gather the Facts

Other than reserving the time and energy to think clearly, you also want to have enough information at hand. After all, the decisions you will make are only as good as the information you have. For example, suppose that you are looking to buy a smartphone. You did some research, but you only found five bad phones. You can take all day to decide which one of them you want to buy, but you will still end up with a bad phone.

But the thing is, you might not have had enough time to gather complete information. Here, you could use System 1 to compensate because you don't have much choice anyway. Still, I recommend that you avoid getting yourself into such a situation in the first place.

So, gather as much reliable information as possible. There's no such thing as "complete" information anyway.

Stay Open to All Possibilities

When we use System 1, we interpret information differently through assumptions. We tend to jump to conclusions or be biased and give more weight behind the information that supports our biases. So, when you need to make an important decision, make sure that you are not using System 1, and stay open to all facts and possibilities, especially those that you do not want or like.

It will be more challenging or even uncomfortable, but it can help you to avoid making the decisions that may satisfy you at the moment but come back and bite you in the future.

Create Rules

Keep in mind that we are all human, so even the best decision-makers are prone to mistakes. We will get tired, unmotivated, rushed, emotional, and stressed at various times. Moreover, it would take forever to gather all the facts and data and then go through each decision in our daily lives.

As such, when the mind is fresh, effective decision-makers often create simple rules and formulas to help guide them in the right direction, and those rules sometimes extend to high-pressure situations. In doing so, you create a checklist of things to do when you need to make a decision, which helps you to remain as objective as possible, rather than relying on intuitive decision-making.

What does this look like when implemented? Think of when you need to make a grocery list. Consider what you really need to buy and stick to it when you are at the store, rather than just browsing from aisle to aisle, being tempted by all the products on sale and your hunger.

Alternatively, you can try to set an upper limit for a big purchase and stick to it. That way, you can stop yourself from buying expensive things that you may struggle to pay for later, such as a big house or an expensive car.

In short, we are all prone to biased and emotional thinking. To minimize this problem, you want to create rules and systems to help your decision-making process.

10 Mind Hacks to Be a Better Thinker

It actually does not take much to be a better thinker. All you need to do is to implement ten of these mind hacks, and you will immediately see improvements in how you think.

1. Trust your gut feelings: as I've mentioned before, the most significant thing that is going on inside your brain is actually in the unconscious section that is often outside your control. It is actually the unconscious mind that does most of the heavy-lifting because this is what filters information we receive from the outside world and then spits out emotions on the other side; we know this as a "gut feeling," and we've always been taught to trust those. Gut feelings are a cross between logic and emotion, because the subconscious mind only follows the system of belief and past experience. You could say that one could replicate gut feelings in the lab. However, it is part of emotion, because of the output. It does not tell us exactly what is wrong, but it tells us that something is definitely amiss. So do not ignore that unsettling feeling when you are about to do something. Your subconscious mind is trying to tell you something.

2. Never think under pressure: again, save the decision-making for later. You're prone to making bad decisions when you think under pressure. So, you want to make some room for your mind to go over the data and available options. But there will be a time when you need to make decisions quickly and with a great amount of uncertainty. What do you do then? Well, try to detach from the situation to give yourself some breathing room. Even if you cannot give yourself the time to think, you can at least give yourself some space by detaching. That means closing your eyes, taking a step back, and taking a deep breath, which allows you to bring your hectic mind to a halt and restart the thinking process.

3. Consider other views: this is a trick employed by many people in a competitive environment to anticipate their opponent's next move. Basically, when you want to make a play, you take into consideration how other players will react. You can also apply it to understand your opponent's strategy and find ways to counter them. Keep in mind that planning is all about considering what could happen, not what should happen. To do this, simply put yourself into the other person's shoes and think as if you were them. What would you do if you were them? Sun Tzu said that if you know yourself and your enemy, you need not fear the result of a hundred battles.

4. Question your preferences: sometimes, your preferences, such as likes and dislikes can blind you to other options. For example, let's say that you love to buy expensive clothes because you have a belief that expensive stuff tends to have a higher quality than the cheaper counterparts. This belief isn't always wrong, but it certainly has flaws. Sometimes, the price for certain products has spiked because of a simple label. A Supreme tag on your shirt won't make it incredibly durable or longer-lasting than its non-branded counterpart. Even if the shirt itself has a higher quality, it probably won't justify its 1000% increase in price. A higher price does not mean higher quality, let alone how much you will enjoy it. Perhaps the fact that you like buying expensive clothes is your brain playing tricks on you. Remember cognitive dissonance? Since you spent so much money on your clothes, you feel the need to justify the price tag, and so you validate your experience even though it is not true. So, what can you do here? Simply figure out what you really like. In our example, maybe the price tag actually does not matter. What matters is that you like to own many articles of clothing and you can start to buy cheaper ones. That way, you can still be happy and save a lot of money in the long run.

5. Take long showers: a shower is a magical place for a bunch of reasons. For one, you always come out feeling fresher than when you went in. But the real magic is the strange phenomena called "shower thoughts." Some say that these thoughts come to you in the shower because you are detached from the world, and so this creates the space that allows your mind to think clearly and properly. You would be surprised to see how some million-dollar ideas come straight from the shower. Most of your shower thoughts will be outright strange. You may wonder, "Why isn't the plural of the word 'pan,' 'pen' when the plural of 'man' is 'men?'" Numerous studies show that you will get these moments most often when you are not aware that you are thinking of the problem at hand. These moments are often when you are taking a shower or a long walk, but since not as many people go jogging or walking at the park, we attribute the source of such thoughts to the shower. This is because the mind does not experience stress or pressure when you are taking a shower or a long walk. When the mind is not under stress or pressure, it starts to think and solve problems on its own.

6. Be skeptical of your memories: what you remember of a past event may not necessarily be what actually happened. Sure, you might be able to recall the general detail of the past with some accuracy, but the smaller details might be muddled. In fact, the more often you recall the same event, the less accurate it becomes. So, basing your decisions on your memories is a bad idea.

7. Don't multitask: the prefrontal cortex is the part of the brain that is responsible for willpower and thoughts. Unfortunately, for something so important, it does not have a large energy reserve. You can tire it out very quickly. For example, suppose that you have to really push yourself into overdrive when you need to complete a project in a pinch; you will tire the prefrontal cortex out. After that, it will be too drained to maintain your willpower, so you are more likely to make impulsive decisions.

8. Learn from your mistakes: we look at successful people as being like a towering building with a beacon of light at the top. The light represents success, and that is the only thing most people see. What many fail to observe is that the beacon is built on top of countless mistakes. Every successful individual will tell you that the key to success is to learn from your mistakes. Many people do not get far in life because they are afraid of making mistakes, but that is the only way to learn and improve. You get a little wiser every time you fail. So be willing to make mistakes and learn from them. Even when you get something right, I suggest that you still look at your performance to see where you can improve. This perfectionism can be unhealthy if overdone, so instead of trying to achieve perfection, settle for incremental improvements instead.

9. Daydream, seriously: daydreaming puts your creative mind to work. Sometimes, you cannot see a solution to a problem until you start to think creatively. Your mind may be muddled already when you try desperately to solve the problem, so you might want to step back and daydream a little to let the logical mind rest and the creative mind work.

10. Think about thinking: think of your own mind as a Swiss Army Knife. It has many uses, but it is only valuable if you know how to use it. Experience or intelligence plays a role in determining your judgment, but this does not matter as much as knowing how to use your mind. The creative, emotional mind may compel you to buy that expensive car, but you want to use your rational mind when you look at the loan terms. So, know which mental tool to use that fits the situation at hand.

Critical Thinking Exercise

Critical thinking is like a muscle. It takes constant practice to improve it. Thinking critically is gathering knowledge and experience. How can we keep improving our critical thinking skills?

How can we encourage people to continue improving their critical thinking skills for a lifetime?

Improving our critical thinking does not need hours of lesson planning or require special materials. Thinking critically yields many benefits, but you just need to be curious and open-minded.

There is no magical way to improve our critical thinking immediately, and it will take time to practice routinely. Below are some strategies you can employ to help you improve your critical thinking skills in your everyday life.

Don't Waste Time

Have you ever noticed in a moment of time that you waste time and realize you get nothing back from it? Everyone has this experience in their lives, even the people who are good critical thinkers. Thankfully, we can maximize productivity and minimize time wasted on trivial matters. For instance, you can take the time you would spend watching TV to plan your days ahead.

We have arranged some questions that you can use to review how you practice your thinking throughout the day:

- "At what points during the day did I do my best and my worst thinking?"
- "What did I think about today?"
- "Did anything come out of my thinking?"
- "Did I allow negativity to cloud my thoughts?"
- "If I could do the day over again, would I do anything differently? What, and why?"
- "Did anything I did or thought have any benefit toward long-term goals?"
- "If I spent the next ten years thinking the way that I did today, would anything important be achieved?"

Spend time going through all of these questions, or just focus on a few at a time and think about your responses carefully, and record it in your journal. The more that you spend time practicing this, the better you will be, and you will see patterns emerging in your thinking habits.

Learn Something New Every Day

Embracing the idea of a lifetime of learning is all about making the process of learning an ongoing journey. You just need to learn something new that you did not know before, on a daily basis. You can start by asking yourself something you have been curious to know. Is there a question about something that you want to get an answer for? If so, go and chase it. Do not stop until you figure out the answer you are looking for. No matter how simple or unimportant the question might be to other people, do not take this into account. From this practice, you can learn two things at the same time. You can fulfill your intellectual need and you can develop your habit of curiosity.

No Boundaries for Learning

Never ever think that you are too old to learn something new or achieve something amazing. There are a lot of famous people who only accomplished great things when they were "old," so ignore your age and start learning to do something new. There is no age limit for learning, particularly in the process of improving critical thinking skills.

Always Question

Asking questions shows a sign of intelligence in your brain. Asking questions means you are curious to know something more. In today's world, we should always encourage our children to ask questions more to discover possibilities and opportunities. Questions are always good, and good questions are always better. The core of critical thinking and lifelong learning is the ability to ask meaningful questions that can lead to constructive and useful answers. Encouraging people to learn by asking questions as the focus will ensure that our learners do not learn in only one way. It is a highly interactive learning process when we exchange ideas and discuss them by asking questions. As a result, we can develop a habit of curiosity by asking questions to look for other opinions and views, taking nothing for granted.

The following questions are used for improving critical thinking skills. Think of something that someone has just told you and after that, ask yourself the questions below:

Who?
- "Do I know that person?"
- "Is that person in power?"
- "Is it important to know who told me this?"

What?
- "Is it a fact or an opinion?"
- "Are all the facts provided?"
- "Is there anything left out?"

Where?
- "Public or private?"
- "Was I given a chance to respond?"

When?
- "Is there any reason for their opinion?"
- "Are they trying to make someone look good or bad?"

How?
- "Happy, sad, or angry?"
- "Spoken or written?"
- "Could I understand?"

Active Listening

Active listening is really essential in critical thinking as you will have enough information from the speaker, and by paying attention, you will come up with good questions that lead to gaining more information. Some say that you have two ears and a mouth for a good reason. A good leader lets others talk first before expressing his or her own ideas and opinions. According to a study from the University of Missouri, many people are weak listeners. It does not help when there are so many distractions, either. Most people think that listening is an easy thing to do, but it is actually very difficult to do, especially when this means active listening. To be an active listener, we need to make a conscious and concerted effort to hear words being said by the speaker, and more importantly, we have to understand what is being said within their message. Moreover, it is also crucial to understand what the speaker wants or is striving to achieve in the conversation.

Improving Active Listening

Active listening skills, like other communication skills, can be learned, accomplished, and taught.

• **Talk less:** this should be obvious because it is impossible to both talk and listen at the same time. Listen and do not try to talk or think of a reply just yet. Focus on what the speaker is saying to get a clear message. After that, you can respond. That way, you allow the speaker to say all that needs to be said so you can fully understand what they are trying to say.

• **Adopt a listening mode:** keep silent and pay attention to hear what they are saying. Furthermore, keep the environment quiet and comfortably open your mind by engaging in eye contact. At the same time, make sure you are responding appropriately. Active listening is meant to promote respect and understanding. When listening, you gain more information, data, perspective, and insights. Attacking the speaker and putting them down does not help anyone. Of course, that does not mean you should just sit there and nod, either. This brings us to the next point.

• **Respond properly:** be candid, honest, and open in your response and assert your opinions respectfully. When you respond and provide your own opinions, keep in mind that you can sound just as wrong to them as they do to you. Remember what is important in the discussion: reaching an agreement on the best solution. So, it does not matter who is right. What matters here is that a good decision has been made that day. Plus, you are here to take in ideas and knowledge, and the other person is there to share it. You can save the discussion until after the presentation. There is always an opportunity to talk.

• **Make the speaker feel comfortable:** you have to show some gestures or signs of agreement in your listening. If you think that seating makes you both feel comfortable, you can arrange the seats for the conversation. Be aware of the environment in which you are communicating.

- **Avoid distraction:** this means you have to make sure that you keep your phone on silent mode, keep the TV screen or speaker off. If the person you are talking to requests privacy, you can hold the conversation in a private room and close the door.
- **Put your personal prejudice aside:** it is difficult for most people, but we can tackle this issue through learning and practice. Interrupting people is considered rude and a waste of time because it only serves to infuriate the other person and restricts a full understanding of the message. Therefore, allow the speaker to finish each point properly. In some cases, the speaker will pause, offering you the opportunity to ask a question. That is the time to speak. Also, never interrupt a counter-argument.
- **Pay attention to their tone:** the tone of the speaker's words can sometimes enhance the meaning of the words, and sometimes, it can hide the meaning of the words. Make sure that you know the difference.
- **Look for the meaning:** when we listen, we will hear what other people say. That much is clear. But what people speak out loud may not actually be what they are trying to say. What we want to listen to is the meaning behind their words, not the words alone.
- **Look for the subtle signs:** it is true that the most observable form of communication is speech, but that only makes up a very small portion of the entire communication process. Everyone communicates through non-verbal languages and cues such as body language, facial expressions, and tone. Look out for those when you talk to people. You might understand what they are actually trying to say.
- **Provide feedback:** communication is a two-way street. You speak, and you listen. But sometimes, when you listen, you may not fully understand what is being said due to personal biases, beliefs, prejudices, assumptions, et cetera. So, you want to counteract this problem by attempting to understand the message clearly. To do

that, you just have to paraphrase what the speaker said. Put their ideas in your own words and verify with the speaker whether you understand what is being said properly. If you are told that you got it wrong, ask clarifying questions. Other than that, make sure to summarize what the speaker said now and again during the conversation, to make sure that you are still on the same page.

Solve Just the Problem

In this day and age, everyone has too many problems to solve and too little time. You may run into various problems everywhere, be it at the workplace, at home, or while you are out and about. I'm talking about the problems that you cannot just sweep under the rug. Some problems naturally resolve themselves, of course, but it's your problem primarily because it came from your actions or choices, and this type of problem does not just go away on its own. So, you are left with only one option, and that is to tackle all problems one at a time and do your best to prevent any more from occurring in the future.

Take a moment now and look at what is wrong with your life. If you find that there are so many things that you lose count, do not despair. This is a very common thing. Even the people who you think have it all figured out also have too many problems that they would rather not think about. But here's the thing, you won't get anything done unless you start to look at your life, see the problems, and start to work on solving them.

You want to build momentum, so you don't have to tackle the biggest problems straight away. You can just start solving a problem so that you can steadily improve your life.

As Les Brown once wrote, "If you have a problem that either a man or God can solve, then you don't have any problem." What he was trying to say was that we all worry too much about the problems in our lives, let alone looking at them and solving them. It's a scary prospect for many people. The thing is that problems are inevitable. They are an aspect of our lives, and we all need to learn to accept this fact. We can achieve more in life if we embrace them and see them just as another chore to cross off the to-do list. Then and only then can we move on to solve problems with a more positive attitude.

Now, let's take a look at one approach mapped out by authors Richard Paul and Linda Elder. In their approach, you will have a roadmap toward solving a problem you need to face daily.

• You have to state the problem as clearly and precisely as you can.

• You have to understand about your problem and know what you are dealing with, and you also need to put aside the other problems that you have no control over and save time to focus on the problems that you can actually solve.

• You need to figure out the information you need and actively discover it.

• You need to analyze and interpret the information you collect carefully.

• You also need to identify what you can do in the short term and long term. Figure out all the options for action and visualize the most appropriate solution you want to happen.

• You have to evaluate your options, and take into account their pros and cons.

• You have to take up a strategic approach to the problem and follow through with it.

• You need to track your progress as you implement your actions and be ready to review and alter your strategy should the need arise. Plus, your strategy should be flexible enough to allow changes when more information is available to you.

It takes lots of time and practice to improve your critical thinking skills, but you will see a significant improvement when you follow all of these simple activities and systems.

Asking the Right Questions

Critical thinking is about utilizing the information that you have to the best of your ability. As such, it is just as important to gather the right kind of information. One way to do that is either by observation or questioning. Observation can only get you so far as it can only answer some of the most basic questions.

Asking the right questions allows you to understand the situation better and analyze it properly. The best way is to follow the "Starbursting method" by brainstorming and asking these six questions: How, what, where, when, why, and who?

For example, suppose that you are tasked with solving an accessibility problem at your office. There have been complaints about the fact that certain stair placements have made it difficult for people with disabilities to gain access to some areas, particularly the main entrance, as it is slightly elevated, requiring the use of stairs. So, the questions you should ask first are:

- **Who:** who is intended to use the stairs?
- **What:** what is wrong with the stairs? What are the options to solve the problem?
- **How:** how can we implement our options? How can we design access in place of the stairs in a way that disabled people can use?
- **Where:** where will we use these new ideas?
- **When:** when do disabled people use the stairs the most?
- **Why:** why do we need to change the stair design? Why do disabled people have such a bad experience?

Alternatively, you can also use the element of thought to help you identify the right questions. Elements of thoughts reflect how we think about the situation. They include purpose, questions, information, interpretation, concepts, assumptions, implications, and points of view.

- **Purpose:** goals and objectives. The question: what are we trying to solve? What do I want to achieve?
- **Question:** problems and issues. The question: what should I need to ask?
- **Information:** data, facts, observations, experiences. The question: what do I need to know to understand the problem?
- **Interpretation:** conclusions and solutions. The question: how do others come up with different solutions?

- **Concepts:** definitions, theories, laws, principles, and models. The question: what is the main concept of this idea?
- **Assumptions:** presuppositions and axioms. The question: what are we assuming to be true or false without confirming?
- **Implications:** results and consequences. The question: how can we implicate these new ideas?
- **Point of view:** frames of reference, perspectives, orientations. The question: how are the different points of view related to the problem?

The next step, of course, is to answer all the questions without any assumptions or prejudices. Here, you should have a deep understanding of the problem, and you can move forward with the steps needed to find the best solution to the problem. In our example here, the solution included using elevators in places where people with disabilities can easily find and access them, or using sloped platforms to allow wheelchair users to go up and down easily.

How to Sharpen Your Logical Thinking Skills

We all know about Sherlock Holmes and his unparalleled logical thinking skills. Thankfully, this is something that we all can achieve with a little practice.

Of course, maybe a convoluted murder case is out of your league, but at least you can improve your logical thinking skills to a level that makes problem-solving and decision-making much easier. These skills will contribute to your success in your personal and professional life. So, what can you do to sharpen your mind?

Learn the Terminology

Before you start brushing up on your logical thinking skills, it is worth knowing the set of associated terms and become acquainted with them—such as assumption, premise, argument, conclusion, inference, observation, different statements, et cetera. That way, the rest of the journey will be much easier.

Making Logical Conclusions

It does sound strange, but practice makes perfect. You do not need to get yourself into a difficult situation to improve your logical thinking skills. Trying to think in conditional statements and finding causes and consequences of small and insignificant facts is enough. Basically, just identify the premise and conclusion in any conditional statement and establish a link between them.

For example, let us assume that if it is snowing, it is cold outside. So, we have the statement: "If it is snowing, it is cold outside." In a conditional sentence, if the premise is true, then the conclusion is also true. That's it. Just develop this kind of thinking with other things and see if the relationship works between the premise and conclusion.

Play Card Games

There are other ways to make the learning process fun. Why not gather your friends once every week to play a light-hearted card game to stimulate your brain to think quickly and logically? Challenging card games will only dampen the mood and make the learning process arduous. Simple card games help improve your memory, focus, and analytical skills.

You can even incorporate strategy into these games to spice things up. Games such as Crazy Eight or Go Fish are perfect for kids. For adults, games such as Blackjack or Poker work just as well.

Make Math Fun

Okay, math is one of the least fun things in the world for many people, but it is also one of the best exercises to improve your logical thinking skills. You see, math is more than just crunching the numbers. Those who excel in math are actually fluent in logic because the only difference between the two is numbers and letters. Math is logic simplified so everyone can make sense of it.

Thankfully, you do not need to sit and crunch numbers all evening to improve your logical thinking skills. There are plenty of fun ways to work on your math. There are plenty of mental challenges in math games on many websites or mobile phone apps that you can access.

Other math-related games, such as Sudoku, are also engaging and challenging, allowing you to improve your brain's ability to solve real problems faster.

Solve Mysteries and Break Codes

Another way to improve logical thinking is by reading crime stories and detective novels. They require logical thinking from readers, after all. If reading is not your cup of tea, consider watching movies or TV shows in that genre instead. The challenge here is to solve the mystery before the hero of the story does. Of course, there will be plot twists or different interpretations of evidence, so do not be discouraged if it is actually different from what you have imagined. What matters here is you get yourself to think logically.

In this case, you often have many possibilities. Your work here is to eliminate those that are improbable or impossible. Another great brain exercise is breaking codes, which you can find on the Internet and play with your friends.

Debate

Debates challenge us to string our thoughts together in a convincing way. While we know something is good or bad, explaining that to others is difficult. Debates force us to search for causes and consequences behind our beliefs, and turn them into strong arguments and find the logical connection behind everything.

Because you need to think logically and decide on the fly, debates can improve your logical thinking skills. So, join a debate club or organize a debate with your friends about literature, society, music, politics, et cetera.

Be Strategic

Logical thinking is all about understanding logical connections and putting the pieces together. By learning how to think strategically, you will develop a valuable asset for both your personal and professional life. Strategic thinking habits include anticipating, critical thinking, interpreting, deciding, and learning. You can improve this kind of thinking by playing strategic games such as board games, video games, or brain-enhancing games or design a strategy for sports events.

Notice the Pattern

Individuals with great logical thinking skills see patterns that others might otherwise miss every day. Those patterns will put their logical reasoning skills to the test, along with the ways that they anticipate and complete them. A great way to train pattern recognition is by scrutinizing everything and finding an answer through an educated guess.

For example, we have a string of numbers: 1, 4, 9, 16, and 25. Which of the numbers below follows?

a) 50

b) 36

c) 44

d) 78

If you chose "b," then congratulations. You noticed the pattern in the numbers. Each number in the string is squared and goes up by one. So, it's 1x1, 2x2, 3x3, 4x4, and 5x5. You need to familiarize yourself with these problems and be able to quickly think of an answer.

Seven Methods of Critical Thinking

"Thinking is skilled work. It is not true that we are naturally endowed with the ability to think clearly and logically—without learning how, or without practicing." A. E. Mander.

Keep Things Simple

Not everything requires a complicated solution, not even all complicated problems. Sometimes, we explain far too much and just end up losing ourselves and others, even down to forgetting what the original problem or question was. Avoid this by going back to basics, back to the questions asked, to try and solve the problem; questions like:

- "What do you know about this already?"
- "How did you know that?"
- "What are you attempting to show, prove, criticize, et cetera?"

- "What are you missing?"

Question Every Basic Assumption

We can all make fools of ourselves by not questioning those basic assumptions. Most scientific breakthroughs began with a challenge to a commonly held belief—innovators simply ask, "What if I was wrong?" Questioning your assumptions will allow you to think more critically about possibilities and about what is appropriate.

Know and Understand Your Own Mental Processes

Humans can think critically, and that is what puts us above other animals. However, it isn't always easy to think critically, mostly because of how we think. The human brain relies, to a large extent, on mental shortcuts, as a way of explaining things happening around us. While that may be useful when you need to make a very quick decision, it may not be so useful when you are making life-changing decisions. Mental shortcuts are not always the most accurate, and that is why it is so important that we are aware of cognitive biases and personal prejudices, because both can affect our decisions.

Yes, all humans have cognitive biases of some description; it's being aware of this that makes us able to think critically and it is something all critical thinkers must consider.

Reverse Things

If you find yourself deadlocked, unable to solve a sticky issue, reverse things. Yes, we know that X is responsible for Y, but what if it were the other way around; what if Y was responsible for X?

The obvious example is the chicken and the egg. Yes, we know that a chicken comes before the egg; the chicken lays the egg, so that is logical. But what if we were to ask where that chicken came from? Well, a chicken comes from an egg, so, surely, the egg comes first, yes?

At times, you will know immediately that the reverse simply isn't true, but it can put you on the right path for the right solution.

Evaluate the Evidence

One of the most useful things we can do is evaluate previous solutions to similar problems, and it is important to do this critically.

If you don't, you can be sure you'll come to the wrong conclusion. Ask yourself a few simple questions—where did the evidence come from? How was it gathered? Why did the other person solve the previous problem in that way?

Take research that was done into sugary cereals, for example. One study, quite persuasively, showed that, in fact, sugary cereals are good for your health. Now, deep down, you know that really isn't true, and when you delve deeper into the evidence, it comes to light that the cereal company paid for the study. In that, it's probably fair to say that that company influenced the study.

However, it would be wrong to write off the result as not being valid; what we should do is keep it in the back of our minds that there may be a conflict of interest.

Think for Yourself

Not everyone has faith in themselves, putting all their trust in reading and research. Often, people forget that they can think for themselves; they forget to use one of the most powerful tools at their disposal—their own minds and brains. Overconfidence is not clever; just understand that, at times, the only way to reach a solution is to think for yourself. Use your own opinions, thoughts, and ideas, and don't just rely solely on other people's.

We Cannot Think Critically All of the Time

It just isn't possible, but you know what? There's nothing wrong with that. Just remember to use critical thinking when it comes to making complex decisions or solving tough problems—you don't have to think critically all of the time and about every single thing.

Six Steps for Effective Critical Thinking

We have to deal with problems on a day-to-day basis, from small and insignificant things to major, life-changing decisions. In many cases, we are challenged to understand a different perspective when we approach any situation. Our thought processes are based on previous experiences or similar situations. While that allows us to think quickly, that does not always mean we can solve problems effectively because our emotions may cloud our judgment. Not only that, our decisions may be further affected by prioritizing the wrong factors, or other external factors as well. Here, critical thinking allows us to establish a rational, open-minded decision-making process that is based mainly on solid facts and evidence.

As we have mentioned earlier, we have developed some mental shortcuts that help us make decisions quicker, especially during life-or-death situations. Here, critical thinking prevents us from jumping straight to conclusions. It may slow down our thought processes, but it helps us to make the right decision. It helps guide us through logical steps that allow us to discover more perspectives and solutions while removing those mental shortcuts that are based on personal biases. The critical thinking process has six steps:

1. Knowledge

Every problem requires a clear vision to see the right solution. In this step, you need to identify the problem. To do so, ask a lot of questions to understand every little thing about the scenario. That way, you can understand what influences the outcome or what you need to address from the start. In some cases, there is no actual problem, so no need to go forward with the other steps. This is just as important, because trying to solve a problem that does not exist is a waste of time and may worsen the situation. To identify the problem, start by asking open-ended questions to gather as much information as possible and pave the way for discussion and explore the problem. The two main questions to be asked are: What is the problem? Why do I need to solve it?

2. Comprehension

After identifying the situation, you can then try to understand the facts and situations that led up to this moment. The information-gathering process should follow any of the research methods that can be changed according to the problem, the type of data available, and the deadline required to solve it.

3. Application

Continuing on from the previous step, this step requires you to connect the dots from the information you gathered to the resources available to solve the problem. You can use mind maps to assist you in analyzing the situation, establishing a connection between it and the core problem, and then determine the best approach to proceed.

4. Analyze

When all the data is collected, and connections have been made between it and the main issues, then the situation is thoroughly assessed to identify: what is really going on; the pros and cons; and challenges to solve the problem. You should focus on the root causes and think of how you can address them in the solution. You can use a cause-effect diagram to help you analyze the problem and its circumstances. The diagram helps you divide the problem from its causes, and to identify and categorize these based on their types and impact on the problem.

5. Synthesis

After the problem is fully analyzed, and all the relevant information is considered, the next step is to decide how to solve the problem and create an action plan. If there is more than one solution, their advantages and drawbacks should be considered. Identify what you need to prioritize to find the best solution in your interest. We recommend you use a SWOT analysis to identify the solution's strengths, weaknesses, opportunities, and threats.

6. Action

The final step is to put your decision into action. Critical thinking also applies in the action phase, and the action should have its own steps. If your action plan is long-term or involves a team, it is worth having an action plan to help you execute your decision properly.

Moreover, your plan should have certain indicators to identify how well the work is going, so you can evaluate your progress and adapt as needed. Of course, your action plan should be clear but flexible.

Other Ways of Improving Critical Thinking

Critical thinking is a process by which we systematically, deliberately if you like, take in information and figure it out for ourselves.

Some of the ways that we can critically consider information include:

- Analyzing
- Conceptualizing
- Evaluating
- Synthesizing

And the information we are thinking critically about can also come from multiple sources such as:

- Communication
- Experience
- Observation
- Reasoning
- Reflection

All of these sources will guide us to have certain beliefs and take action.

Critical thinking is not the way that we regularly think every day. At certain times, we happen to think automatically, but when we think deliberately, we use some of the critical thinking tools and skills to reach a more accurate conclusion.

Most of our thinking every day is not critical, and that's good for us because we do not have to spend a lot of our brain energy thinking about everything. If we had to think about everything critically or deliberately, we would not have any cognitive energy left to think of something else that is more important. Thus, it is good that much of our everyday thinking happens automatically.

However, we can run into problems if we let our automatic mental processes govern important decisions. If we do not think critically, it is easy for people to control us. In our everyday life, if we fail to stop and think deliberately, it is easy for us to get caught in pointless arguments or involved in silly things.

The Six Thinking "Hats"

Your thinking style has its own pros and cons. Optimistic thinkers often see the chances, but tend to overlook risks or downsides associated with them. Cautious thinkers are the opposite, seeing only risks and not opportunities. By changing up your thinking style, you may be able to find new solutions to tricky problems.

The best way to approach a problem is by viewing it from various angles. You can use the "Six Thinking Hats" model to help you adopt different viewpoints. It can also be used as a decision-checking tool in group situations, because you can encourage everyone to explore the situation from many perspectives simultaneously.

By forcing you to move away from your habitual thinking style, the Six Thinking Hats model allows you to look at a situation from a different perspective, allowing you to view it more objectively.

While you can think up a good solution to your problem using a rational, positive viewpoint, it is still worth exploring the problem from other angles. For instance, you can view the problem from an intuitive, creative, emotional, or risk management viewpoint. You may be surprised to see what good solutions you are missing out on. Plus, not deciding based on these viewpoints can mean making a decision that is poorly received by others because their needs are not met, creative ideas are not used, or essential contingency plans are not acknowledged.

Implementing the Six Thinking Hats Model

This model may be used in team meetings, for example, by giving every hat to every person evenly, or individual hats to individual people. In this setting, there is the benefit of preventing confrontation because each person sees the same problem but from a different angle; that means everyone has a valid opinion—each hat is equal to one way of thinking.

White Hat

White hat is a thinking style that primarily focuses on the available data. You look at what information you have, analyze past trends, and try to spot a pattern or learn something from it. Try to find gaps in your knowledge and try to account for them or fill them. You mustn't proceed further than comprehending the facts and knowledge gap. The questions here are: "What do we know?" and "What data do we have?"

Red Hat

Red hat focuses more on intuition, gut feeling, and emotion. The objective of this thinking style is to understand the emotional reaction from everyone without trying to understand the reason behind those reactions. Most importantly, try to understand the responses coming from those who do not understand your reasoning. Here, you should ask, "What do you feel about this suggestion?" and "Does anything feel off for you?"

Black Hat

Black hat is more about what negativity can come from a decision. Everything must be looked at from a defensive or cautious standpoint; rather than seeing the way it can work, look at where it won't work, where things can go wrong. Critically, this type of thinking can show where a plan has weak points, giving you the option of elimination, making changes, or having a plan in place to counter the negative outcomes.

With black hat thinking, your plan can be more solid, because you will see the risks and the flaws before implementation. By the time you implement the plan, it would be too late; resources will have been expended, and you will be too far in to get out unscathed. Lots of highly successful people exhibit over-optimism, and this leaves them wide open because they do not see the issues ahead of them. They are not prepared for anything to go wrong. Ask yourself, "Is there a way for this to go wrong?" and "What risks are there?"

Yellow Hat

Yellow hat thinking is positive, sunny thinking, represented by the color of hope. Optimism helps you to find the benefits in your decisions, to see what values they hold. This type of thinking is motivating, especially when the going is hard. You should ask yourself, "What advantages does this solution hold?" and "Why is this solution a viable one?"

Green Hat

Green is the color of intelligence, and it is representative of a creative streak. With this hat, your approaches to a problem should be creative, promoting free-thinking and little chance of criticism.

Blue Hat

This style of thinking focuses mainly on process control. It is intended to guide the whole decision-making process and determine which "thinking hat" everyone should use. So, when things go wrong, the blue hat will be used to go through the entire process to diagnose what is going on and then apply the correct thinking hat to solve that problem. If it finds that the problem is the lack of ideas, then the green hat will be used. If you find that things go wrong and contingency plans need to be created, the black hat will be used.

An Example of Six Hats

So, how does it look when the six thinking hats are used? Of course, not all of them are needed in most scenarios and which hat you use depends on the aim of the decision. This thinking model can also be used in another context. For example, it can be used to help students develop their creative thinking skills and learn how to identify solutions after they have developed an in-depth understanding of the problem.

To illustrate how these hats would be used, I will give you two scenarios. In the first scenario, different people in the team will utilize different thinking hats to make a decision. In the second scenario, everyone puts their minds together under the same thinking hat but then switches the hat as they go through the decision-making process.

Scenario 1

So, in the first scenario, suppose that you are one of the directors of a property company. The board is considering whether they should invest in a new office block. Preliminary research shows that the economy is flourishing, and there is also a high demand for office spaces because they are being bought left, right, and center. So how would the six thinking hats be utilized in this situation?

Let's start with the white hat. Here, some directors look at all the data they have. In this case, they look at their supply, which is the vacant office space available in the city. Due to the economy, they see that the vacant office space is already starting to go down. If they decide to get the new office building now, then by the time it is built, the supply will be extremely low. Other than that, they also see that the economy is growing, and they expect the growth to continue.

Next, some other directors put on the red hat and look at the current building design. They say that the current design looks dull and does not inspire creativity and productivity, and also point out that the company's previous customers made the same complaints, as well as the fact that the competitors are also switching up their design to something more modern.

Then the black hat thinkers come into play. Here, they look at the economic forecast, and they know that it can be wrong. What if the economy were to experience a downturn suddenly, then all the office buildings would just sit there rotting away, or be only partly occupied for a short while, which means no profit. If that happens at any point in the future, then everyone is looking at an economy with high supply and low demand.

On the other hand, the yellow hat thinkers understand that there are always risks associated with any investment. It will be a huge money sink, but they are more optimistic about the economy. If it is still flourishing and the forecast is correct, then they stand to get a high return on investment. They also acknowledge the danger of an economic downturn, but they suggest various contingency plans to counteract this effect. They can sell the office buildings before that happens or continue to rent them out but on longer-term leases that could last through any recession. This makes renting the office space a very appealing prospect for many businesses, even if the buildings themselves aren't aesthetically pleasing.

Next, the green hat thinkers take the advice from the red, yellow, and black hat thinkers and consider whether they should redesign the building. They have a few ideas here. They can go for the prestige design that looks so appealing that people would still want to rent the space even during the economic downturn, even if it means spending more on the construction. Alternatively, they can take advantage of the recession as the office building costs would go down. Then, they can simply buy out those properties, sell or rent them out after the recession, both of which would yield a high return on investment.

Throughout the process, the blue hat thinkers control how the discussion goes and ensure that ideas continue to flow and encourage other directors to change their thinking hat models and see if they can come up with more ideas.

When you put all of these thinking styles together, the board of directors has a much clearer idea of the situation and its possible outcomes and can make decisions accordingly.

Scenario 2

This time, you are in a group of designers who are tasked to redesign your company's product package. The flow then would be something like this:

First, everyone puts on the white thinking hat to discuss what they know about the package. What does it look like? How do our competitors design their packages? What do the customers say about our package? How well-received are the packages of our competitors?

Then, everyone proceeds to the yellow hat thinking to identify the advantages of redesigning the package, its process, and how the product can benefit from the new design. So, you can ask about the benefits of the redesign or what positive impacts would the new design bring.

From there, the whole team puts on the black thinking hat and looks at the disadvantages of the design change. They discuss the negative impacts on product sales and marketing targets. Here, everyone looks at the risks associated with the design change.

Everyone then proceeds to the red hat thinking, reflecting their emotional reactions toward the current package and the new one. How does everyone feel about the current package? How does it compare to the new one? What might the customers feel toward the new design? How does the team feel about changing the current design?

In the green hat thinking phase, everyone starts to think of the new design from a creative and innovative perspective. This helps the team think about the new design, and they can improve upon the previous one by looking at its design flaws.

Throughout the entire decision-making process, the moderators wear the blue hat to keep the ideas and discussion going and direct it in a way to facilitate the session.

As you can see, the Six Thinking Hats model allows us to view a situation from various standpoints, giving us the chance to analyze the situation further to gain an in-depth understanding. Moreover, this model also provides us with a systematic thinking method by covering the topic from different approaches. This kind of organized thinking can lead you to an ideal solution in the decision-making process.

Conclusion

Thank you for reading *Cognitive Biases: A Fascinating Look into Human Psychology and What You Can Do to Avoid Cognitive Dissonance, Improve Your Problem-Solving Skills, and Make Better Decisions.* With all of the knowledge acquired from this book, you are well on your way to improving your thinking skills and identifying your own biases, and hopefully, learning to be a little less prejudiced.

The key here is to think systematically and go slow if you must. It is always better to think slowly rather than to decide incorrectly. Having good critical thinking skills puts you way above others professionally and personally, as you can decide and act in a way that best benefits everyone. One cannot stress how important it is to develop your critical thinking skills, especially in this day and age, where manipulation and misinformation run rampant.

Thankfully, you are no longer a victim of these falsehoods. Your life will be significantly improved thanks to your new way of thinking. Pat yourself on the back for reading this far, and good luck on your journey.

Resources

Part 1:

https://www.verywellmind.com/lesson-three-brain-and-behavior-2795291

https://www.sciencedaily.com/releases/2018/11/181108142443.htm

https://opentextbc.ca/introductiontopsychology/chapter/3-2-our-brains-control-our-thoughts-feelings-and-behavior/

https://www.huffpost.com/entry/20-psychological-studies-_n_4098779

https://www.mindful.org/mind-vs-brain/

https://en.wikipedia.org/wiki/Heuristic

https://examples.yourdictionary.com/examples-of-heuristics.html

Part 2:

https://en.wikipedia.org/wiki/List_of_cognitive_biases

https://en.wikipedia.org/wiki/List_of_fallacies

https://blog.hubspot.com/marketing/common-logical-fallacies

https://www.boardofinnovation.com/blog/16-cognitive-biases-that-kill-innovative-thinking/

https://www.inc.com/jessica-stillman/6-cognitive-biases-that-are-messing-up-your-decision-making.html

https://www.randstad.ca/employers/workplace-insights/women-in-the-workplace/how-to-subvert-unconscious-biases-at-work/

https://hbrascend.org/topics/how-to-manage-biased-people/

https://blog.iii.ie/inside-track/5-ways-to-reduce-unconscious-bias-in-the-workplace

https://greatergood.berkeley.edu/article/item/how_adults_communic
ate_bias_to_children
https://www.newsweek.com/parenting-parents-mom-dad-biased-
favorite-child-research-study-finances-equal-677768
https://mcc.gse.harvard.edu/resources-for-families/5-tips-for-
preventing-and-reducing-gender-bias
https://www.forbes.com/sites/pragyaagarwaleurope/2018/12/03/unco
nscious-bias-how-it-affects-us-more-than-we-know/
https://www.thoughtco.com/gender-bias-4140418
https://www.sciencenewsforstudents.org/article/think-youre-not-
biased-think-again
https://www.theguardian.com/women-in-
leadership/2015/dec/14/recognise-overcome-unconscious-bias
https://www.psychologytoday.com/us/blog/in-practice/201508/6-ways-
overcome-your-biases-good
https://www.fastcompany.com/90303107/how-to-become-a-less-
biased-version-of-yourself
https://hbr.org/2015/05/outsmart-your-own-biases
Part 3:
https://www.verywellmind.com/what-is-cognitive-dissonance-2795012
https://www.drnorthrup.com/4-ways-to-reduce-cognitive-dissonance/
https://en.wikipedia.org/wiki/Neuroplasticity
https://www.designorate.com/steps-effective-critical-thinking/
https://highexistence.com/its-all-in-your-head-how-to-take-advantage-
of-neuroplasticity/
https://collegeinfogeek.com/improve-critical-thinking-skills/
http://www.skilledatlife.com/how-beliefs-are-formed-and-how-to-
change-them/
https://www.briantracy.com/blog/personal-success/10-step-process-to-
solve-any-problem-critical-thinking/
https://www.forbes.com/sites/forbescoachescouncil/2018/10/09/overc
ome-biases-and-blind-spots-in-decision-making/
https://www.psychologytoday.com/us/blog/persuasion-bias-and-
choice/201806/5-tips-better-decision-making

https://www.realsimple.com/work-life/life-strategies/10-ways-better-thinker

https://www.mindtools.com/pages/article/newTED_07.htm

Printed in Great Britain
by Amazon